"This book came to me just as a group o[...]
asking, 'How can we develop a healing prayer ministry?' I can't imagine a more thoughtful and practical resource than *Experiencing Healing Prayer* by Rick Richardson. Even where readers may differ with the author, they'll find honesty and sensitivity and experience on every page."

BRIAN MCLAREN, PASTOR AND AUTHOR OF *A GENEROUS ORTHODOXY*

"This is a very practical book that is also the very personal story of a journey in the Spirit. Rick Richardson has not only learned much that is helpful, but he has picked up great gifts of communication along the way. I was greatly encouraged as I read this work. I felt excited all over again about praying for the sick, distressed and marginalized. The teaching points that Rick makes as he tells his story have equipped me to feel that my journey will now be that much more effective."

STEVE SJOGREN, FOUNDING PASTOR, VINEYARD CINCINNATI, AND WRITER OF <www.servantevangelism.com>

"*Experiencing Healing Prayer* is one of the most thorough books on healing prayer I have seen. It's not just a book about healing, however. It's a great book on how to grow deeper in discipleship and prayer. It's full of life-changing insights into our relationship with God, ourselves and others."

STEVE NICHOLSON, SENIOR PASTOR, VINEYARD CHRISTIAN CHURCH OF EVANSTON, AND NATIONAL COORDINATOR OF CHURCH PLANTING FOR VINEYARD CHURCHES USA

"Rick Richardson paints a compelling portrait of effective healing prayer ministry. His is a balanced and biblical view of such ministry, one that emphasizes listening to God, obedience to God, and reliance upon the healing power of a loving and sovereign Father. Through his transparency about his own journey of healing, he invites us to open ourselves to deeper possibilities of God's healing work. I recommend this book highly."

STANTON L. JONES, PROVOST, WHEATON COLLEGE, AND COAUTHOR OF THE GOD'S DESIGN FOR SEX FAMILY SEX EDUCATION BOOK SERIES

Experiencing Healing Prayer

HOW GOD TURNS OUR HURTS INTO WHOLENESS

Rick Richardson

InterVarsity Press
Downers Grove, Illinois

InterVarsity Press
P.O. Box 1400, Downers Grove, IL 60515-1426
World Wide Web: www.ivpress.com
E-mail: mail@ivpress.com

InterVarsity Press® is the book-publishing division of InterVarsity Christian Fellowship/USA®, a student movement active on campus at hundreds of universities, colleges and schools of nursing in the United States of America, and a member movement of the International Fellowship of Evangelical Students. For information about local and regional activities, write Public Relations Dept., InterVarsity Christian Fellowship/USA, 6400 Schroeder Rd., P.O. Box 7895, Madison, WI 53707-7895, or visit the IVCF website at <www.intervarsity.org>.

All Scripture quotations, unless otherwise indicated, are taken from the Holy Bible, New International Version®. NIV®. Copyright ©1973, 1978, 1984 by International Bible Society. Used by permission of Zondervan Publishing House. All rights reserved.

Every effort has been made to secure permission for copyrighted material. Any additions or corrections will be made in future printings.

Design: Cindy Kiple

Images: man looking at beach: Juan Silva/Getty Images
         woman praying: Barbara Penoyar/Getty Images
         various prayer photos: Rick Franklin and Andrew Craft

ISBN 0-8308-3257-2

Printed in the United States of America ∞

Library of Congress Cataloging-in-Publication Data
Richardson, Rick, 1955-
  Experiencing healing prayer: how God turns our hurts into
wholeness
  / Rick Richardson.
     p. cm.
  Includes bibliographical references.
  ISBN 0-8308-3257-2 (pbk.: alk. paper)
  1. Spiritual healing—Christianity. 2. Adjustment
(Psychology)—Religious aspects—Christianity. I. Title.
  BT732.5R53 2005
  248.8'6—dc22
                                                                    2004029842

P	19	18	17	16	15	14	13	12	11	10	9	8	7	6	5	4	3	2	1
Y	19	18	17	16	15	14	13	12	11	10	09	08	07	06	05				

Contents

Foreword

To write a book about healing is a formidable task. It is so easy to lose focus and balance, becoming shrill and dogmatic while over-promising or making healing a form of Christian magic. Rick Richardson has avoided all these pitfalls and given us a rich, nuanced, thoughtful, experience-based, story-filled and practical guide to the healing ministry. He is able to do this because he sets healing in its proper contexts.

First of all, he understands healing to be an aspect of Christian transformation, not just relief of symptoms (though it often results in this). He sets healing in the context of the real issues of postmodern people: addiction of all sorts, gender issues, mother and father wounds, sexual trauma, marginalization. (This is a profoundly post-modern book that will touch our postmodern generation.) He sets healing in its primary context, which is God, God's presence, God's whispered word, worship, liturgy and the sacraments. He under-stands healing to be a journey toward wholeness that involves listen-ing prayer, healing of memories, forgiveness, laying on of hands, use of images, service to others and so on.

This is a practical book. Richardson provides simple yet powerful healing exercises at the end of many chapters. He also gives the reader a step-by-step guide to beginning a healing ministry, including guidance in how to teach others to pray as well as outlining the process of engaging in healing prayer with others. Richardson is also well aware of the dangers of a healing ministry. Chapter seventeen, where he deals with these issues, is alone worth the price of the book. In fact, all who engage in ministry of any sort should read this chapter.

Finally, this is a book that not only teaches but also evangelizes because it touches people at the places where the Spirit can work—those dark points of brokenness, longing, pain, disadvantage and injustice. Rick has written a book that sets evangelism in its proper context, which is spirituality and transformation.

Richard Peace, Ph.D.
Robert Boyd Munger Professor of Evangelism and Spiritual Formation,
Fuller Theological Seminary

Acknowledgments

I would like to claim originality for all that follows. But I would be remiss if I did not acknowledge the immense debts I owe to C. S. Lewis, Dallas Willard and especially Leanne Payne. Lewis suggested the philosophical approach that I use. Willard developed that approach in relation to life in the Spirit. Payne applied these insights to the ministry of healing and prayer.

As I wrote this book, I often felt like a child at play in the castles of giants. The people at whose feet I sat were as much beyond me as the realities they describe were beyond them. I was humbled and often sensed my own smallness. But I also learned that playing in the castles of giants is a worthy pastime. My soul can't help but expand when I look above and beyond me. Maybe you'll find that to be true too as we play together in the giants' castles.

I am deeply thankful to others who often joined me in these higher climes and who gave invaluable feedback on the manuscript, including Kevin and Karen Miller, Sandy Beelen, Doug and Marilyn Stewart, and my outstanding editors, Andy Le Peau and Ruth Goring. I am also thankful to all my colleagues at InterVarsity Press and at InterVarsity Christian Fellowship—especially Geri Rodman, Mary Anne Voelkel and all those with whom I have partnered these many years in the Urbana Missions Convention prayer effort.

I am also deeply indebted to those others with whom I play on a daily basis: my kids Chris, Steve and Colby, and especially MaryKay, my sweetheart and favorite friend. Without their support, not only this book but even a reasonably healthy life would be far beyond my reach.

Finally, I want to acknowledge the immense debt I owe to my own parents, Dick and Pat Richardson, who have also become friends over these last years. Their example, love of life and vision for contributing to their world has shaped me in ways too numerous to mention. It is to them that I dedicate this book.

Introduction

One year when I was in high school, my friend Dan bamboozled me into going to Ocean City, New Jersey, for a spring-break week of fun and sun on the beach. What I didn't know was that each evening there would be speakers who would challenge us to commit our lives to God. Midweek, Jay Kesler spoke. He was the president of the trip's sponsoring organization, and his challenge to come home to God moved me deeply.

I will never forget the soul struggle I engaged in that night. I knew if I returned home a Christian believer to my highly educated family, which was sometimes quite hostile toward simple faith, I would not get a warm reception. But at three in the morning I came to the end of my struggle and met my God face to face. My life has never been the same.

The next afternoon I joined others to hear my group leader talk with some two hundred folk hanging out on the beach about how to begin a relationship with God. In the middle of his presentation, he crooked his finger and beckoned me over. I didn't want to go. But I did. When I got to where he was standing, he thrust his microphone in my hand and invited me to tell what God had just done in my life. Haltingly, even incoherently, I began to speak.

After a few minutes, our leader invited all who had decided to become a Christ follower that week to join him in the surf. He baptized forty of us that afternoon, amidst the turbulent ocean waves.

What a beginning!

Later in college I got "the rest of the story," as Paul Harvey likes to say. I learned what it means to follow God. I grew through studying the Scriptures, praying daily, having fellowship with other people of faith and sharing my experience with people still outside God's family. Those were good times of growth. It was as if God had an umbrella over my head or a spiritual Teflon coating around my life. I failed often but was so full of enthusiasm that it didn't seem to matter. Only later did the cracks in my soul begin to appear, and widen, and sometimes split open, revealing seething emotions and a confused heart.

The crisis crystallized in my thirtieth year. I had just moved to Chicago with my wife and our two-year-old. I felt stressed and lonely. Nobody knew my name or cared about my work. I became driven to turn things around, to please authority figures and to become known. I was living in an anxious workaholism. My wife and I began to feel less close to each other, and we drifted toward the edge of danger in relationships outside our marriage. I was lonely but was away too often to feel connected to her. She was lonely but too hurt to seek comfort from me. At night I was haunted by recurring dreams filled with images of tornadoes out of control, crashing waves, violent men.

Seeking help, my wife and I joined a small group and began to pursue the soul's journey toward healing. We had three mentors in our group. Our first mentor, C. S. Lewis, taught us through his writings to understand our true self, our true identity in Christ. Our second mentor, Leanne Payne, leader of a prayer ministry and author of a number of books, was teaching us about the presence and power of God with us to save and to heal. And we were seeing the life of our third mentor, Jesus, with new eyes, realizing that because the kingdom or rule of God had come in his life and ministry, we didn't need to be trapped in self-destructive patterns. Jesus set so many people free when he walked the earth. He is a master in the art of healing the soul and the body.

One night as I went to bed I was troubled by a mental image of a man I had known years earlier. In my mind's eye he was coming at me with a knife. The image was so powerful that I tossed and turned for several hours before being able to fall asleep. When I awoke, the image returned with a haunting reality. I told no one.

Later that day I met with William, my prayer companion from the small group. As soon as we began to pray, he looked up and in a quiet voice reported that he was seeing a man coming at me with a dagger. He asked if that image meant anything to me. I related my experience of the night before and told him about my long-ago relationship with this man. In his understated way, William remarked, "Maybe God wants us to pray about that relationship."

That prayer session began a profound healing process in my masculinity and my relationships, especially with men. I experienced the healing touch of God and the blazing light of his wisdom. I invited Jesus into my heart and my imagination in ways that touched and transformed me at the core of who I was. That prayer time was such a turning point that I will return to it several times in the pages to come. Suffice it to say now that I came into touch with some divine resources for soul healing that I had never before experienced.

For a number of years I have worked with college students and people in their twenties. Many of them are trapped in hidden temptations, addictions, negative emotions, self-centeredness and sin. Their study of Scripture, their prayers and all their attempts to psyche themselves up to do right don't seem to be working. Alcohol, addictive sexual experiences or dependent relationships trap them, or they are fighting a losing battle with depression or self-hatred or hopelessness or anxiety or fear. And they aren't finding much help anywhere. Struggles like theirs are increasing as families break down and society gropes for a moral foundation. The need for healing has never been more urgent.

Look around you. How many trapped and hurting souls do you know? How helpless have you felt as people confess their pain and brokenness, looking for some help or relief? How helpless have you felt when you've needed a touch from God in your own life?

This book is about the soul's true journey into healing. We can enter into and experience Jesus' ministry of healing and transforming souls. Do you want to join me on this journey? Let us walk a while together.

A word on how to use this book: You can work through it on your own. But your experience will be even more profound and powerful if you take this journey in a small group or with another person. The end of each chapter provides discussion questions and a simple healing prayer to use personally or with others

May God guide and bless our journey together into healing.

Invitation to the Healing Journey

I will never forget that Sunday morning. We had been preparing to pray for people in the worship service. Several months earlier Bill Leslie, senior pastor of LaSalle Street Church, an inner-city congregation, had shared his desire that our church become a place of deep healing.

As I write these words, memories of Bill Leslie flood my mind. Philip Yancey, who also attended LaSalle at that time, speaks for me in a memorial reflection he wrote about Bill years later:

> Bill talked too loud in the pulpit, and laughed at his own oft-repeated jokes, and he occasionally slaughtered the English language. But he was our pastor, and we grew to love him.
>
> Bill Leslie did many things wrong, but he got one thing right: he understood the grace of God. He recognized his own endless need for grace; he preached it almost every Sunday morning; he offered it to everyone around him in starkly practical ways. Because of his faithfulness, the Near North side of Chicago is a very different place today. And so I believe is heaven.[1]

Bill drew me into his lifelong vocation of seeking and extending grace. He recruited me to lead the healing prayer team that ministered at LaSalle Street Church. That first Sunday Bill preached on the woman who had a hemorrhage that had lasted for twelve years. You can read about her in Mark 5. Because of Jewish purity laws, her condition kept her isolated from others, and the Gospel writer tells us that she had suffered at the hands of many doctors. Still, she believed if she could just touch the hem of Jesus' robe, she would be healed. She did, and she was.

But Jesus didn't let her slip away anonymously, still a social pariah. He wanted to heal her fully. So he looked around for her, exclaiming that he had felt power go out of him when she touched him. Finally she identified herself, and he spoke these powerful words: "Daughter, your faith has healed you [made you whole, or as in some translations, 'saved you']. Go in peace and be freed from your suffering." Bill wove his own story of brokenness and healing into his telling of this woman's story.

At the end of the sermon, Bill looked out at the congregation earnestly and offered the opportunity to come forward for prayer. He had a wonderful way of putting the invitation. "The worst that can happen to you is that you will have an experience of being profoundly loved. And that's not so bad, is it? And you might hear the Master's voice, 'My son, your faith has made you whole. My daughter, your faith has made you whole. Go in peace, freed from your suffering.'"

People streamed forward. We prayer ministers prayed for them in teams of two. The prayer time lasted nearly thirty minutes. And such prayer ministry, launched on Mother's Day 1986, continues today on the second Sunday of every month in LaSalle Street Church.

All of us long to be healed. We know things are not as they were meant to be, neither in our individual lives nor in our common lives as churches, communities and even nations. We long for things to be put right.

The healing ministry is about letting God put things right in our lives.

HEALING FOR SEXUAL, RELATIONAL AND SOCIAL HURTS

In our world the healing ministry is urgently needed. We live in a day of immense challenge and incredible opportunity. Divorce is at an all-time high. Broken and blended families and single-parent households are more and more the norm rather than exceptions. Gender confusion and sexual addiction are becoming epidemic. Historically, pornography and compulsive masturbation were male problems, but in our incredibly sexualized culture, increasing numbers of women are also struggling with these problems. The Internet has made addictive experiences available at the touch of a mouse.

At a recent Urbana Missions Convention I led a prayer seminar on sexual healing and purity for twenty-five hundred students. A staff team of seventy prayer ministers had been trained and stood ready to pray for the students. The sexual struggles people brought seemed overwhelming. Cross-dressing, demonization, homosexual struggles, addiction to pornography, sexual abuse, compulsive masturbation, widespread promiscuity, intensely sexualized fantasy lives and debilitating emotional dependencies are just a few of the many issues we prayed for. If God doesn't stretch forth a powerful hand to heal and save, where are we headed as a culture, as a world? Sexual and relational brokenness, woundedness and confusion rage among us, maybe as much in the church as in the broader culture. Can God make a difference? Can God's power and presence heal us? If not, how real and potent is the gospel? Is it really good news?

The wounds for which we need healing are not limited to sexual and gender identity and experience. Today's young people drive the entertainment, fashion and media industries, and they live in a horizontal culture of peers who decide morality and values without much regard to former generations and older authority figures.[2] Trust in institutions and leaders has been shattered. Further, ethnic divisions and hatred are tearing the world apart. Violence is increasingly pervasive and being exported to the world through mass media.

Who will deliver us from such a divided world? Who will inter-vene to halt the global violence? Is God still powerful and present to heal and to save? Is the good news really good?

In the face of all these challenges, I remain profoundly hopeful. God is still at work. Jesus is still the same Jesus. What Jesus did in the Gospels and in the biblical book of Acts, God can and will do in our day. God is powerful and present to heal and to save, if we will but open our eyes and our hearts and look to God in faith.

I also have profound confidence in the emerging generation. Yes, there is increasing brokenness—sexual, relational and emotional. But there are signs that the emerging generation could lead the way into a new day of healing and transformation in the church and in the world. This generation is more relational, more experiential, more naturally spiritual, more rooted in worship and in mystery. Young people today are also more vulnerable and authentic with their pain and their reality. Thus I believe that the emerging generation is poised to turn to God to humbly seek healing. And it is poised to lead all of us into the healing presence and ministry of our transforming God.

WHAT'S IN A NAME?

At the heart of our search for healing is our longing for a transformed identity, an identity that is solid. Think of all the identity labels we throw around—gender, class, racial and sexual orientation labels. We seem to believe that if we can find the right label, we have found our identity. Our culture has become so confused and self-referential in the search for the source of human identity. *We try to name ourselves.* This act of self-naming may be the most central characteristic of the spirit of our age. But we can never name ourselves. The effort is doomed to failure from the start.

The journey of healing is at its heart a journey of hearing and embracing our true name, our deepest identity. It is about becoming who we were created to be, reaching all the immense and beautiful potential that we have because we are made in the image of God and therefore of infinite value. We need to hear our true name. We need to hear from our Creator who we are and how valuable we are. Naming ourselves is a futile activity. But as we turn to God to name us, God can lead us into a new future full of transformational possibilities.

What do you face? Have you struggled with sexual addiction, or gender confusion, or an intensely sexualized fantasy life? Have you experienced sexual abuse? Are you part of a broken or blended family or a single-parent home that left you longing for more parental nurture, blessing and protection? Have you experienced broken relationships that wounded you deeply?

Do you find yourself numb, apathetic or emotionally flat? As you were growing up were you mistreated or abused, physically or sexually? Are you emotionally dependent and unhealthily enmeshed with another person? Is violence a primary part of your inner world, your entertainment world or your outer world? Are you part of an ethnic community or marginalized group that has experienced discrimination or rejection? Do you have a physical condition that you would like God to touch and to begin to heal?

If you resonate with any of these common struggles, this healing journey is for you. If you long for God to put things right and know that God is our only hope, then this healing journey is for you.

I invite you to join me in the journey. The worst that can happen is that you will have an experience of being profoundly loved by God and by others you invite to be your traveling companions. That's not so bad, is it? And the best that could happen is that you might hear the Master's voice: *My son, your faith has made you whole. My daughter, your faith has made you whole. Go in peace, freed from your suffering.*

When I was considering whether to write this book, and if so what it should look like, I spent some time in the gardens at Cantigny west of Chicago. As I pondered, I had a sense that the book would be not so much an academic exploration as a heart-to-heart conversation. I would receive healing in the conversation and so would you.

So let us walk for a while together in the garden of the heart and talk about things of the soul. Let's travel together on the healing journey toward wholeness in Christ.

2

What Is Healing?

What does the healing journey look like? What is healing? How much healing can we expect?

I recently tuned my television to a Christian station. A well-known evangelist and healer was speaking right through the TV set to his viewers. He talked about God's power to heal and told how mightily God had worked in a recent event. The camera panned a large audience and ended at a stage. People gave testimonies of healing and then were directed to demonstrate that they had been healed. Next they were "slain in the Spirit," which meant that the healer touched them and they fell over, presumably under the influence of God. I couldn't tell if the healer had just shoved them over, if they had swooned or fainted, or what had happened.

The camera's focus came back onto the evangelist, who seemed to look straight through it at his viewers. He asked us if we had received our miracle. If we would just have faith, we would certainly receive it. And our faith could only be strengthened if we would financially support the evangelist's ministry. After all, God gives to us far more than we can ever give to God—and of course giving to this evangelist was giving to God.

I was both attracted and repelled. I was attracted to the possibility that sufferers were being helped. But I was repelled by what felt like manipulation. If someone wasn't healed, it was said to be their own fault. They didn't have enough faith. That sure let the evangelist off the hook! It wasn't his fault if they weren't healed. With that explanation, people who weren't healed now knew that they were not only sick but also pathetically weak because they lacked faith. To me that didn't seem helpful. Further, the unabashed tying of faith and healing with money made me very skeptical about what might be driving the operation. Is that what healing looks like? Is that a good picture of the healing journey?[1]

At the other end of the spectrum, the following week I listened to a preacher who argued with great passion that the spiritual gifts of healing, prophecy and others listed in the twelfth chapter of 1 Corinthians have ceased. They were only for the first generation of Christians, who overlapped with the era of Christ's time on earth. He claimed that people and ministries still practicing these supernatural gifts and expressions of God's Spirit are deceiving themselves and dabbling in the demonic.

But preachers who preach against the gifts and the ministry of healing seem to have little to say to encourage strugglers and hurting people who are gripped by pornography, sexual addiction, depression, self-hatred or physical illness. "Buck up, be a man, suck it up and endure" is about all this preacher seemed to be able to offer. Is the healing journey merely a never-ending cycle of self-effort, doomed to fail if the wounds in our souls are deep and devastating?

- Healing is the most important thing for Christians; it happens all the time and is often dramatic and complete.

- Healing is for a bygone era, so buck up, mate, and get through it.

However, I have daily conversations with people whose beliefs lie between these two extremes. They believe God *can* heal but rarely does. They follow Jesus, love God and do their best to fight their inner demons and pain. But their life is marked by defeat, depression and even despair over the hidden, persistent inner struggles of their soul. They lack joy, victory and a sense of the reality of God's healing presence.

What does the healing journey look like? What is healing? How much healing can we expect?

Since so many people have such varied opinions on these questions, I owe it to you to start with what I believe about the healing journey and what approach I will invite you to take. To share my heart and my perspective on healing, I want to take another look at the mission and ministry of Jesus.

JESUS' MISSION IN LIFE

Healing was absolutely central to the mission and ministry of Jesus. It was at the heart of what Jesus was all about. And since we are followers of Jesus, his message and ministry still need to define *our* message and ministry.

Jesus summed up his message in life when he said, "The time has come. The kingdom of God is near. Repent and believe the good news" (Mark 1:14). I need to unpack his statement just a bit.

"The time has come" was an announcement about the time of the fulfillment of God's plan for human history. In Greek the word translated "time" is *kairos*. *Kairos* refers to special time, in contrast to the other Greek word for time, *chronos*. *Chronos* means clock time. *Kairos* means special time, the appointed time, the time of fulfillment.

"Kingdom of God" is the defining description of the whole life and ministry of Jesus. Understanding what he meant by "the kingdom of God" is crucial, then, for understanding everything Jesus did and said.

For Jesus' original hearers, "the kingdom of God is near" meant that God was about to intervene in human history to establish God's own rule and fulfill the divine plan for Israel. In Israel's Scripture, what Christians call the Old Testament, the prophets like Isaiah, Jeremiah, Zechariah and Daniel all looked forward to a time when God would deliver Israel from all its oppressors and enemies. God would then rule Israel, and through Israel the world, making Israel a light that would transform all the nations and draw them to God.

To usher in God's rule, Jesus proclaimed the nearness of the kingdom of God and then proved just how near it was by healing the sick and casting out demons. For the people of that culture, sickness and spiritual oppression were interrelated realties that demonstrated how pervasive Satan's rule was in the world. Jesus showed that Satan's dominance had ended and that people would now be freed from sin, sickness and spiritual oppression.

Then things started to go wrong. Certain expected events—God's intervention, expulsion of Roman oppressors, vindication of Israel, and the establishment of God's rule on Mount Zion in the Hebrew temple—never occurred. Instead the rulers of Israel rejected Jesus, advocated his death and asked the Roman leaders to crucify him. To say the least, these events did not follow the script that most Jews expected the Messiah/deliverer to follow. It looked as if Jesus' ministry to usher in God's rule had totally failed.

A DIFFERENT WAY

It turned out that God had a different way forward, not as cataclysmic as Israel expected. Rather than invading and overwhelming history, God chose to work *within* history, through individuals and a community, to establish his kingdom. Jesus' death and subsequent rising were the inauguration of God's kingdom. This kingdom would now expand throughout human history through the community that identified with Jesus.

We, God's people, press into human history and into our world the kingdom or rule of God. We proclaim Jesus, just as Jesus proclaimed God's kingdom. And then we validate the message by following Jesus in his ministry of healing the sick and casting out demons. These ministries show our contemporaries that people are continuing to be freed from sin, sickness and spiritual oppression. Our healing and deliverance ministries may look different from that of Jesus, because for people and nations in our time different things may be seen as signs of God's breaking into history. But make no mistake, God's people still proclaim Jesus' kingdom message, pursue Jesus' kingdom mission and practice Jesus' kingdom ministry.

We also follow Jesus on the way of the cross and resurrection. We suffer because people who have a lot invested in the old order never like the inbreaking kingdom of God. For all of us, God's rule compromises our own attempts to rule. As Milton's Satan remarks, we would rather rule in hell than serve in heaven. We would rather stay sick and in control than be healed and lose control.

The Christian message is the cross: judgment is pronounced on old ways of doing things and seeing the world, and they must die. Jesus' message was never just about becoming nice.[2] It is about being made new through death to the old ways and resurrection to the new.

Jesus' message of freedom from sin, sickness and spiritual oppression would have lost its vitality long ago if he had not *shown* us how real it was in the lives of those to whom he ministered. And our message of freedom from sin, sickness and spiritual oppression loses credibility and currency unless we also minister freedom from sin, sickness and spiritual oppression. Jesus' ministry of healing is far from done; it is as crucial as ever. We, his followers, carry it on.

But how?

A few biblical passages will show us how Jesus healed and how

Paul, the apostle, talked about the ministry of healing. Some of these insights are what you would expect, but others may surprise you.

HEALING IN THE GOSPELS

In John 9, Jesus encounters a man born blind. Jesus' followers get busy trying to figure out who's to blame for the man's blindness. Was it his parents' sin or his own? Jesus tells them that neither the parents nor the man were the cause. This man was born blind to give glory to God through being healed. In other words, Jesus doesn't pick apart the past and try to assign blame. Jesus looks ahead to the future and to the good God can bring out of a tragic situation.

Jesus spits on clay, rubs it on the man's eyes and sends him to wash his eyes off in a pool nearby. The man does so and goes home seeing.

Friends and neighbors are puzzled, and many don't believe it's the same guy who was blind. But he insists that it's really himself! So these friends and neighbors take him to the religious leaders. Maybe they can make sense of what has happened.

The religious leaders are not fans of Jesus, to say the least. Jesus cares about people a lot more than about rules, and he cares about healing the hurting and broken a lot more than he cares about appearances. So Jesus keeps breaking religious rules. He has healed on the sabbath when he isn't supposed to. He brings dirty, unkempt, hard-drinking, hard-living people to God, folks who wouldn't have been caught dead in the synagogue or temple—or if they *had* been caught in the temple, they might have been *made* dead.

So the formerly blind man is set up for confrontation with the religious people. They want to make him swear that it wasn't Jesus who healed him or that he isn't really the formerly blind guy or that even though Jesus healed him, Jesus is from the devil. The blind man gets exasperated with these religious leaders and finally observes that they're so obsessed with Jesus that they must want to become his followers too. At that point he is excommunicated from the synagogue, rejected by his community.

Notice a couple of things. First, the man is healed on several levels. His eyes are healed but so are his willpower and courage. He is healed physically *and* spiritually. The fullness of the healing is clear when Jesus finds him later and he readily acknowledges Jesus' identity and worships him. Jesus practices a whole-person approach to healing.

Second, in some ways Jesus lessens the man's pain and suffering, but in other ways Jesus puts him in a position to suffer and feel pain even more. *Healing is not primarily about escape or relief from pain,* at least as Jesus practiced it. This is a great challenge to us: I think most people pursue their own healing and minister healing to others with the primary goal of finding relief and release from pain. That's the wrong goal, at least from a biblical perspective. Healing is primarily about the transformation of the person into a truer and more whole follower, worshiper and lover of God.

Sometimes the healing journey raises us up onto mountaintops where we feel the sun and the wind, the exuberant joy of wider horizons and clearer perspective. And sometimes the healing journey leads us through the shadow of death, the valley of loneliness and darkness. In the end we are transformed to be like the One who healed us. But at points along the way, our pain and darkness may increase as we take a turn toward wholeness.

My friend Dave can testify to this. He was addicted to pornography. Underneath his addiction was a deep anxiety related to early loss of his mother's love. He felt intense inner pain and covered it up by turning to Internet porn. As soon as he began to seek healing and sought prayer and accountability for his addiction, he had to start facing the intense anxiety that he had been covering up. It was a *very* painful time. But through prayer, God's presence and loving community, he experienced profound healing.

For Dave, the way to life and freedom from addiction passed through the darkness of facing his inner emptiness. When he no longer had pornography to comfort him, at first he felt greater pain. But then he was able to receive what he really needed, real love and nurture from real people, rather than the substitute that pornography had become. The journey toward the mountaintop of healing often leads through the dark valleys of our past experiences of pain and trauma.

Wholeness in Christ, being transformed to be more like him, is its own reward. But it doesn't always feel like a reward. Sometimes it feels more like a punishment, a wrong turn, a mistake. The man born blind could certainly testify to both sides of the healing coin. He was more whole—but he also suffered as a result of being true to Jesus.

Let's look at another healing experience in the Gospels, the one mentioned in chapter one of this book. In Mark 5 Jesus heals a woman who had been hemorrhaging for twelve years and had suffered a great deal under the care of doctors, spending all she had. The doctors had made her worse, not better! In addition, her bleeding made her unclean, a social outcast in her community,. The loneliness must have been intense, and the feeling of being flawed must have gone to the core of her being, marking her indelibly with shame.

She hears about Jesus and his healing ministry and thinks that if she can just touch his cloak she will be healed. She does, and immediately she feels the bleeding stop and the discomfort drain away. For the first time in twelve years she feels good physically. Is her healing complete? Not by a long shot.

Jesus *feels power go out of him* when the woman touches his cloak. That's an interesting phrase. Jesus' body and even clothes were channels of God's healing power. The language of healing is a language of *flow*.

So Jesus looks to see who has touched him. And his followers once again get busy correcting him: in such a large crowd Jesus must be out of his mind to wonder who touched him. What a nonsensical question with so many people jostling against him!

Jesus, as usual, tunes out the clueless disciples and keeps looking around. The woman finally comes forward and admits what she had done. She is trembling with fear. She has broken the rules of social contact: she, an unclean pariah, has touched a holy man.

How surprised she is when Jesus speaks words of affirmation and blessing! "Daughter, your faith has healed you. Go in peace and be freed from your suffering." Jesus knows she needs not only physical healing but profound emotional and spiritual healing too. She needs to be sure. She has been taught to feel ashamed of who she is because of her illness. Jesus tells her it is her faith that has brought healing. She is to be commended, not rejected. And she is free of the bleeding. She can fully rejoin her community. Her healing, then, is also *social*. If she had slipped away without her healing becoming public knowledge, she would have remained ritually unclean and outcast.

When I read about this event, I am deeply moved. This woman was healed on every level of her being. She experienced physical healing, healing of her sense of self, healing of her spiritual self-image ("your faith has healed you") and healing of her social relationships. That's the way God heals. If you explore the many other healing experiences recounted in the Gospels, you will find the same pattern. Jesus sought the wholeness of the people to whom he ministered, not just a respite from physical suffering.

You may also have noticed that this woman was freed from her suffering and pain. Is this inconsistent with the earlier account of the man born blind who was freed from physical suffering only to face a different kind of suffering? I don't think so. The key issue is not relief or release from pain but *transformation of the person toward wholeness in and through Christ.* For the woman, transformation at this point in her life meant a release from suffering. Jesus met her and healed her in the ways she most needed in order to move toward wholeness in God.

THEMES OF HEALING IN PAUL'S WRITINGS

Now let's examine some of the explanations of healing in writings of the apostle Paul. If healing is movement toward wholeness in Christ, then there are some crucial passages where Paul talks about the healing journey.

One comes in his letter to the church at Ephesus (Ephesians 4:20-24). Our union with Christ, says Paul, has given us a new identity, which he calls our new self. We first put off the old self—old patterns and ways of thinking, without God and without hope, locked in self-centered absorption. Then we are renewed in the attitude of our mind by reading Scripture, by good conversation with others, by healing and by prayer. We put on the new self, which is our true identity in Christ. We put on, and grow into, wholeness in Christ.

Healing is an inside-out deal. We are transformed from the core of who we are. As we experience and live out that transformation, we are healed on every level. Watching as persons are healed from the inside out has been an amazing experience for me. Inside-out healing often affects people in very physical ways: I have seen spines straightened, headaches lifted, ulcers calmed and even eyes healed. These physical dimensions of healing were outward and visible evidences of deep emotional, spiritual and soul transformation.

Some people in healing circles make a big distinction between physical healing and "inner healing" or emotional healing. I don't make such a sharp distinction. The goal is wholeness in Christ, which means being transformed into the image of Christ that each of us is meant to reflect uniquely. Thus healing invariably affects all dimensions of our being. Whenever we pray for another, we seek to address root causes of any broken, wounded or sinful part of the person. We want to minister to people so that they grow in freedom from sin, sickness and spiritual oppression into the image of Christ that they uniquely are meant to bear. Sometimes that wholeness will involve dramatic physical healing and sometimes not.

Paul gives us a wonderful summation of the healing journey: "And we, who with unveiled faces all reflect the Lord's glory, are being transformed into his likeness with ever-increasing glory, which comes from the Lord, who is the Spirit" (2 Corinthians 3:18). In the end the healing journey is the larger life journey of being transformed into the wholeness of the image of Christ.[3]

Of course the ministry of healing will lead us to address hurts, wounds and brokenness, with the goal of freedom from their damaging effects. We long to see people freed from suffering, and we seek out all that God has for us in the healing of our souls, emotions, minds, wills and bodies. But as we seek healing and freedom from suffering, we keep the ultimate goal uppermost in our minds and hearts. For ourselves and for those we pray with, we want nothing less than transformation into the image of Christ.

At the same time we remember that complete wholeness in Christ will be ours only when Jesus returns and we are changed in an instant to be like him. Wholeness is the destination, but we will finally and fully get there only when the kingdom that Jesus promised is fulfilled. So we are patient with these decaying bodies and fragile souls. Even so, the kingdom of God has invaded history, the Spirit is active, and progressive transformation toward wholeness in Christ is the birthright of every person who has become a follower of Jesus.

At the end of most chapters in this book you will find reflection questions or a prayer response. You can use these questions and prayer for your own healing journey, but they will be even more powerful and helpful if you are working through this book with a small group of people, discussing the questions and praying the prayers in community. Community is a helpful context for many of the steps in the healing journey. So consider if there is a person or persons you can ask to join you.

You may also want to begin keeping a journal of your insights and of what God says to you or does in you as we carry on our conversation in this book.

FOR REFLECTION AND RESPONSE

1. In what ways might stereotypes of healing and healing ministries, like those noted at the beginning of the chapter, keep people from trusting God to heal them?

2. How do you respond to the definition of the healing journey as the journey toward your unique wholeness in Christ?

3. In what ways have you already experienced healing in your life?

4. In what ways would you like to see God heal you as you work through this book?

5. Spend time praying for wholeness in Christ, for you and for others.

A Map for the Journey

On any journey we need a map.

To get to many places we can choose among different maps and directions with varying amounts of detail. But in the Western world today it can be hard to find a map for the soul's true journey toward healing. How does healing happen? What is the soul? What is the soul's destination? How do we get there? In a very materialistic and pleasure-oriented age, questions like these are not asked very often. But if we are ever to make the soul's journey toward its true home, we will need a map and a reliable set of directions.

There are signposts along the way on the healing journey. This chapter points out some of these signposts. The rest of the book will help you learn to apply them to your own life and the lives of others.

What is the first important signpost along the way toward the healing of the soul?

In the introduction I told how I saw a mental image of a man coming at me with a knife. I told no one about this troubling image but went that day to pray with my prayer companion, William. He practiced the first key to the healing of the soul. As he *listened* for the still small voice of God to lead him, he saw an image of a man coming at me with a dagger. It was the same image that had so haunted me the evening before.

William took a risk by telling me what had come to his mind. What if the image meant nothing to me? He would have looked a bit foolish. But he described the image, it connected for me, and we entered into a time of healing that was life-changing. William had learned to listen to the whispering voice of God's Spirit. You can too.

Chapter four will focus on the substantial reality of God's healing presence and why collaborating with what God is already doing can have a powerful impact in our lives. In chapter five we will learn how we can invite and practice God's presence for healing. Then in chapter six we will learn the principles of hearing the whispering voice of God for ourselves and for others. Listening prayer is at the core of the art of healing the soul.

> **SIGNPOST 1**
> **Learn to practice God's presence and to hear God's still small voice.**

As you struggle with emptiness, loneliness and pain, these chapters about the being and nature and voice of God may seem a little tangential at first. But soak up all you can from these chapters. They will help you recover the vitality of God's presence and being. They will help you look up and out of yourself to God, from whom all true healing comes.

So what's the second signpost on the healing journey?

That image of a man coming at me with a dagger wrapped up some of my fears and images of men and masculinity. I have struggled to come to a healthy self-image as a man, and I have not always known how to express masculine energy and power in a balanced way. For instance, I am afraid of anger. Part of my journey has involved learning the power and goodness of righteous anger and masculine strength.

What's more, I have had distorted images of God as Father. I have seen God as authoritarian and uncaring in his use of power. I have been horrified at Old Testament pictures of God as judge. And I have not easily embraced Jesus' ability to cleanse the temple and "kick butt" among the commercial moneylenders who were keeping the Gentiles from worshiping God. My distorted images of men, the masculine, of God as Father and Jesus as judge have kept me immature in my life with God and others. My responses to authority figures have been confused and confusing. At points I have been too oriented toward them, desperately needing their approval. At other points I have been harshly judgmental, projecting falsely negative motives and actions onto authority figures. For those to whom I'm accountable, supervising me has been a challenge!

Have I had worse experiences than most people? No. As a matter of fact, I have had many wonderful experiences with men and masculinity (and with women and femininity). Throughout the book I will be exploring the healing and shaping influences of people like my mom and dad, who were in many ways very good parents and to whom the book is dedicated. But of course my parents were fallen people, and my journey has included healing in relation to them. We live in a fallen world, and all of us are fallen and sinful people. Most of us need some degree of healing to gain freedom from sin, sickness and spiritual oppression in relation to our parents. This book is therefore for all of us, however healthy or broken our family and cultural experiences were. And in the healing journey, our imagination matters.

At the heart of many of our struggles, especially ones related to sexuality and gender, are our images and past experiences of men and masculinity, women and femininity. We need new images. We need our imagination cleansed and renewed by God's Spirit. Even our memories need healing for us to relate healthily to women and men around us. Often I have prayed with people who have very little capacity to see God as a loving parent or to relate to God as a benevolent authority. Until these people's fundamental images of father, mother and authority figures have been healed, their capacity to relate positively to God is often very limited.

> **SIGNPOST 2**
> Replace diseased images and memories of God and human beings with healed and transformed images.

The best way to bring healing to the soul is to let the Spirit of God work in our mental symbols, memories and imagination. The human imagination wraps up intense, complex truths in powerful and poignant images. If God can transform these mental symbols, God will have done much to heal our heart. Mental pictures can give us access to issues and past events that are otherwise hard to address. Counseling can lead us to talk our feelings round and round without any ultimate relief or change. But when our images of men and masculinity, of women and femininity, and of God are transformed, and we live accordingly, *we* are transformed.

What's more, our imagination gives us access to our most painful, anxious experiences and feelings in a way that allows *objectivity* in the healing process. Talking about feelings can lead us into self-absorption, enmeshment in an anxious, subjective inner world. But working with our images and memories gives us a foothold to climb out of the miasma of painful, anxious emotions. We can look at our past and our mental images with an objectivity and distance that help us immensely in the healing process.

Images and the imagination matter! At its heart the healing of the soul involves the healing of the diseased, distorted images we carry of God, others, our world and ourselves. If God can heal our images, he can heal our heart. This truth is our second signpost; it will be explored further in the seventh chapter and the rest of the book.

Let's continue with the third signpost on the healing journey. One of our primary and defining mental images is our *self*-image. The healing of the soul is in part the healing of the image we have of ourselves. We need to come into a healthy sense of personal identity.

The Scriptures tell us a lot about who we are. One of the great thinkers about human identity was the apostle Paul, who planted churches all across the Roman Empire in the decades after Jesus walked the earth. In chapter 4 of his letter to the Ephesians, Paul says, "You were taught, with regard to your former way of life, to put off [one-time act] your old self, which is being corrupted by its deceitful desires; to be made new [ongoing act] in the attitude of your minds; and to put on [one-time act] the new self, created to be like God in true righteousness and holiness." What is the new self we are to put on? And what is the former way of life we are to put off?

The new self is our real identity in Christ. The old ways of life could also be called our "false" or "fleshly" identities. We are to renounce and put away from us the false identities that we have cultivated and that the world system feeds. And we are to put on and embrace our real identity in Christ.

What is a false or unreal identity? I don't know about you, but I have struggled often with an inner dialogue that other people don't hear but that affects my life a lot. Certain self-doubts often surface when I enter new situations. I have a perfectionist internal voice that tells me I never quite make the grade. I have a competitive side that is always pushing me to believe the lie that if others win, I lose. And I have an anxious self that worries that I will never have enough money, security or love. These inner voices want control. They want to drive me and others crazy with endless activity to meet insatiable needs.

Many of these voices come out of inner beliefs that just aren't true, beliefs about myself, my world, my relationships and my God. These voices urge me to live out of a false identity, an inadequate personal identity. They tell me I am worthless, unlovable, threatened, insatiably needy.

How do I break into that inner barrage? How do I discern and reject the lies these voices tell? How do I renounce the false selves and voices? How do I learn and embrace my real identity, based on a realistic view of my self, my world, my relationships and my God?

> **SIGNPOST 3**
> **Renounce unreal identities.**
> **Discern and embrace your**
> **real identity.**

Chapters eight and nine delve into how God sees us and the unique name God gives to each of us. These chapters also teach us how we can identify and transcend those neurotic, dependent, anxious voices and selves that seem so real to us.

The next signpost on the healing journey may be the core of it all, the fork in the road that stands out the most as we look back.

When I was a kid my dad often told bedtime stories to my brothers and me. One of my favorites was "Boots and His Brothers" by Peter Christen Asbjornsen. A king had a castle on a high hill. It shared the hill with a massive tree whose roots went deep. The tree was magical. Every time someone tried to chop it down, it grew.

Because of the castle's location, the water supply had to be carried in buckets for a mile up the hill. So the king made a proclamation: whoever could chop down the tree and channel water uphill to the castle could have the hand of his daughter in marriage and be king after he died.

Many tried to chop down the tree, but it kept growing and growing. Finally the king decreed that anyone who failed would be killed.

The tree had gotten so big and its roots reached so deep that it was breaking the castle wall. After that, many men tried, failed and died.

Finally three brothers started off from their farm far away to take up the challenge of the tree and its roots. On their journey, the youngest found a magic ax that could chop at the speed of light, a magic spade that could dig at the speed of sound and a magic walnut that gave water in a never-ending stream. He set the ax chopping, the spade digging and the walnut gushing, and so he solved the problems of the king and his castle. Of course, he got the girl and they lived happily ever after in a room with a view and plenty of fresh, clean water.[1]

The key to defeating the magic tree was getting all the way down to its roots. As long as the tree had its roots, it would continue to grow and break apart anything in its proximity. Chopping at its branches actually made the problem worse. Until the roots could be dug out, the tree would flourish, resisting all attempts to end its dominance.

Many of our attempts to heal the soul are similar. We focus on the trunk or the branches, the symptoms of our problems. Under a cloud of depression, we try various ways to just feel better. But these comfort strategies relieve the darkness for only a while, and then the darkness is back, often worse than before. Addicted to sex or pornography, we focus on willing ourselves not to do it or on repressing the feelings and images we have in our heart. And guess what? Our problem gets worse. Burdened with self-hatred or constant anxiety, we try to figure out what it is about ourselves that we hate or what it is that we are anxious about at the moment. If we could change ourselves or our situation, the anxiety or self-hatred would lessen. But our anxiety grows and our self-criticism sharpens. We hate ourselves for hating ourselves! Feeling needy and dependent on another person, we think that if we could just change our feelings toward that person or get them to love us in just the way we need, we would feel fulfilled and healthy again. It doesn't work.

If we focus on the symptoms of our knottiest problems, the problems will probably get worse. But if we can uncover the roots of our problems, God can begin to heal us in the right place.

That's true in our own life. It's also true in our ministry with others. We must get at the roots, and not just the fruits, of the problems and pains people confess to us and those we face ourselves.

Often the roots of our problems and pain lie in our earlier years, in our primary relationships. Whether you have experienced abuse, addiction, depression, anxiety or fear, you will find many of the roots in the early part of your life. If you merely focus on the symptoms, you will find little help. But as you get underneath to find the source of your fear, anxiety or depression, God can heal your soul. Chapters ten through fourteen will help you get at the roots of your problems and pain.

> **SIGNPOST 4**
> **Get at the roots of pain and problems, not just the fruits or symptoms.**

There is a fifth signpost on the healing journey.

Five years after God began to heal the images of men and masculinity that I carried in my soul, I began to focus on the healing of my images of women and femininity. I attended a healing conference led by Leanne Payne, whose teaching on gender, and especially on mother and the feminine, is truly profound.

The last day I went forward for a prayer of commissioning and blessing. I went to Anne, my friend William's wife. She laid hands on my head and then my heart. She prayed a prayer of deep blessing and feminine nurture. I felt warmth and light entering my soul. She anointed my forehead with oil as a sign of God's Spirit with me, and my forehead and lips burned with a sense of the presence and calling of God. She fed me Communion, and my body and soul felt nourished and strengthened. Then she gave me a parting hug, a holy hug, which mediated the nurturing, radiant love of God. I walked away washed and renewed, full of a sense of feminine nurture and love, ready to pour myself out for the nurturing of others.

What happened in that precious time of prayer was a work of God's Spirit. But God's Spirit used bread and wine, oil, the hands and arms and soul of a woman filled with nurturing love. God used matter and flesh. God healed my soul through very physical and symbolically powerful channels.

We people of faith tend to have too disembodied a view of God's work. We don't really understand the Christian teaching of the incarnation. God became flesh, and there are absolutely stunning implications for how God heals and works in the world. God loves matter. He made it. God fills and uses matter to heal. That's why the laying on of hands is important. Our flesh becomes a channel for God's Spirit. That's why Jesus mixed saliva and clay to heal a blind man. That's why handkerchiefs taken from Paul the apostle to the sick brought healing (see Acts 19). That's why in James 5, elders are commanded to anoint the sick with oil when they pray for healing.

The fifth signpost toward healing is use of the material and human means God gives us to minister healing. Chief among these are the sacra-

> **SIGNPOST 5**
> **Use the physical and sacramental means God has given as channels of healing power.**

ments. The Communion celebration ought to be the greatest healing service any church has to offer. Baptism ought to help bring cleansing, healing and deliverance from any addictive force or oppressive pressure in our life. God has provided resources beyond belief for the healing of the soul. Often we ignore those resources. No wonder many among us are sick in mind, body and soul. It doesn't have to be that way.

There's a final signpost. When ministries of healing have a powerful initial impact on people and then run dry or get off track, it's often because they have neglected this part of the journey.

Many people become locked in a constant search for a new healing experience, and then they become very frustrated at how slowly they move forward after the initial "conversion" experience. We can be like little children whose constant refrain is "Again! Again!" Instead we are to grow into maturity. As we are being healed, as soon as we are able we must turn our focus outward. In the end we walk into our real identity through following God, living out of God's love, drawing on God's wisdom and building healthy relationships. We do not acquire our true identity through accruing cool spiritual experiences, however helpful and encouraging they may be.

> **SIGNPOST 6**
> **Turn outward! Healing that empowers compassion and service in the world is true healing.**

Healing prayer is not primarily a means of relieving or escaping suffering. Primarily healing is a way of becoming conformed to the image of Christ, who gave his life away for others. We are healed so that we can imitate Christ and bring honor to God. We are empowered by our healing to grow in compassion and minister to others. That's the real point of the healing God works in our soul. God sees our suffering and has compassion on us. But he has a much bigger vision for healing in our life than we do. God does not just want to relieve us from our painful feelings. Much more, God wants to help us to enter into the significant work of becoming agents of healing and reconciliation in our world. He wants us to be what we were each uniquely made to be, to give to others in a way that will bring deep joy to God, to us and to those we serve.

This turn outward is crucial! I have seen too many people's healing stall and abort. They never transcend the narcissism that is prevalent in our culture and especially tempting for those of us who have suffered emotional deficits. From my perspective, the last state of seekers who insatiably hunger for repeated healing experiences is worse than their first state.

Certainly there are times when God calls us to focus inward. We have to grieve losses that can never be fully recovered, and for a time our grieving can use up immense energy and focus. But these periods of grief and inner work are for a season only. Many people who enter such a season are tempted to remain in their inner world for much too long. The antidote is to reach out and focus on the needs and struggles of others, to express God's presence and power and minister healing and love in the lives of those around us.

A friend on a prayer team that I served with for ten years was struggling in the course of one conference. As she grew up she had received very little nurture or presence from her mother. She often struggled with a deep sense of abandonment. God had brought much healing to her, but as the conference leader invited people to receive prayer from the prayer team, my friend felt she had absolutely nothing to give. In obedience to God she took her place and listened to and prayed for people as they came to her. As she gave what little she had and asked God's presence to minister through her, a miracle happened. The empty place in her was filled as she focused outward, on the needs of others. She had come to this most crucial signpost in the healing journey.

I think the first followers of Jesus had this experience of being healed and filled as they took a step to give from what little they had. The feeding of the five thousand recounted in every one of the Gospels is a wonderful analogy of just how crucial the turn outward is. There are many ways we can choose to turn outward. We will focus on a few of those ways in the book's final chapter.

Let's revisit our signposts on the healing journey.

SIGNPOST 1
Learn to practice God's presence and to hear God's still small voice.

SIGNPOST 2
Replace diseased images and memories of God and human beings with healed and transformed images.

SIGNPOST 3
Renounce unreal identities. Discern and embrace your real identity.

SIGNPOST 4
Get at the roots of pain and problems, not just the fruits or symptoms.

SIGNPOST 5
Use the physical and sacramental means God has given as channels of healing power.

SIGNPOST 6
Turn outward! Healing that empowers compassion and service in the world is true healing.

My prayer is that God can use our journey together to restore and renew these turning points in your life and ministry and bring profound healing to you and through you. May God love this broken world through you and me!

FOR REFLECTION AND RESPONSE

1. What signposts in the healing journey from this chapter have you experienced in the past? How have they helped?

2. What signpost in the healing journey from this chapter do you think you may need to experience? Why?

3. Spend some time in prayer. Ask God to use this journey to bring great healing to you and through you.

4

The Healing Presence of God

Every Wednesday night the church I was part of had a healing service. We gathered in a little Episcopal church on Route 59 in West Chicago. We worshiped wholeheartedly for at least a half hour. Then someone would give a thirty-minute teaching on healing based on a passage from the Gospels. Finally, we would invite people for prayer.

In the beginning only a few people came. But over several years the healing service grew to fifty or sixty every Wednesday night. People came in hurting, discouraged, anxious, weighed down by sinful choices and the grief of broken relationships. They left with the weight lifted and with hopeful and refreshed hearts.

Sometimes I needed to be ministered to, and at other times I prayed for others who were broken and burdened. Years later we all looked back at that simple service as a transformational experience that sparked hope and healing in us. Many who eventually became leaders of that church were initially drawn to the church and trained for ministry and leadership through the Wednesday-evening service.

During that period the church grew from 75 people to 350 people, with the healing service as a crucial catalyst.

What was so powerful and profound about that service? Why was God so at work? What melted our hearts and prepared our spirits for healing?

Two dimensions of that service stand out, even ten years later. We worshiped until we knew God's presence was there tangibly with healing power. And then we waited, as a group and in prayer with individuals, until we sensed the nudge of God for what to pray for and how to pray. In other words, we practiced the healing presence of God and waited to hear God's still small voice. In that environment, healing descended on our hearts like a dew of refreshment, nurture and strengthening.

SIGNPOST 1
Learn to practice God's presence and to hear God's still small voice.

SIGNPOST 2
Replace diseased images and memories of God and human beings with healed and transformed images.

SIGNPOST 3
Renounce unreal identities. Discern and embrace your real identity.

SIGNPOST 4
Get at the roots of pain and problems, not just the fruits or symptoms.

SIGNPOST 5
Use the physical and sacramental means God has given as channels of healing power.

SIGNPOST 6
Turn outward! Healing that empowers compassion and service in the world is true healing.

In the next few chapters we will explore how we can practice God's healing presence and hear God's still small voice. In this chapter I want to spark your longing to experience the healing presence of God. Healing begins with lifting our eyes off our pain and anxiety and beholding the glory of the real presence of God.

St. Augustine prayed, "Set love in order in me."[1] The healing journey is the journey of *setting love in order.* We love some things too much, inordinately. We love other things too weakly. In general we love things too much and God's presence and voice too little.

Some of us feel our desires are too strong, sometimes out of control. Lust or neediness, depression or anger, can frighten us, threatening to overwhelm us.

In his remarkable essay "The Weight of Glory," C. S. Lewis challenges us to consider that our desires may not be too strong but too weak:

> We are halfhearted creatures fooling about with drink and sex and ambition when infinite joy is offered us, like an ignorant child who wants to go on making mud pies in a slum because he cannot imagine what is meant by an offer of a holiday at the sea. We are far too easily pleased.[2]

Above all, we are to love God. Just as important, we are to love our neighbor as ourselves. These greater loves will in the end push out or set in place our lesser loves. As we learn to love and long for God and practice God's presence in more focused and ongoing ways, we will progressively be set free from the distorted, inordinate passions and lusts that can overwhelm our little lives and fickle hearts.

This chapter is about learning to love and long for God and God's healing presence. When we acquire a taste for feasting on the presence of God, other loves are set in right relation to this supreme love. We can come to love other things with an appropriate love, with perspective on the things of this world, free from the addictive power of inordinate love. There's more to it than that, of course. But this is the beginning of the healing journey.

When we are filled with God and his healing presence, we are filled with the power that set the stars in the heavens and the planets on their courses. Such power can transform a whole universe—how much more a human life.

Do you long to be filled at the core of your being with more strength, more substance, more hope? You may feel urgent need of immediate help and practical steps. But I implore you to realize that knowing God, practicing God's presence and seeking God's life are more important for your healing than anything else in all the world.

PEOPLE OF THE PRESENCE

To explore the power of God's presence, let's start by looking at Moses. Moses had a laserlike focus on the importance of the presence of God for his own life and the life of his nation.

Moses, the biblical leader of Israel, faced a daunting challenge: to lead the disparate and often despairing tribes of Israel through the desert to the Promised Land. Israel was God's beloved but exasperating child. God had delivered the Israelite people from bondage to Egypt and led them into the desert around Mount Sinai to worship God. God had done astonishing miracles to deliver Israel. But as soon as Moses had gone up onto Mount Sinai to listen to God's voice, Israel began to forget God. After a little over a month the people were making their own gods out of gold and worshiping these gods in orgies of drunkenness and lust.

God's judgment came upon Israel through Moses. Then God told Moses that God would send his angel along with Israel through the wilderness but couldn't send his own presence. Israel was just too fickle. The people were not ready to be that close to God. God is love, but God is not sentimentality. God is pure love. God hates it when people do things that are self-destructive and self-absorbed. God consumes such self-centeredness with God's fiery presence.

Moses couldn't agree to let God remain absent. His prayer in Jewish Scripture, in the book of Exodus, stands as a beacon prayer for all time for those who want to learn to walk in the presence of God.

> If your Presence does not go with us, do not send us up from here. How will anyone know that you are pleased with me and with your people unless you go with us? What else will distinguish me and your people from all the other people on the face of the earth? (Exodus 33:15-16)

Moses tells us the distinguishing mark of our humanity as we follow God and are being healed: we are people of the Presence.

Later on Moses illustrates the results of being people of the Presence. Whenever he spent time in the presence of God and then came out to the people, his face glowed! The presence of God changes even our appearance. Further, when Moses went up on the mountain again to talk with God, he was there for forty days and forty nights without any food or water (Exodus 34:28). How was this possible? Apparently Moses feasted on the presence of God, which turned out to be satisfying and substantial enough that Moses could do without food and water.

THE MOST REAL THING WE EVER ENCOUNTER

The substance and satisfaction found in the presence of God were objects of reflection for C. S. Lewis. Especially in his book *Miracles,* Lewis challenges our present-day conceptions and images of God's Spirit. For those who live in the modern world, the spiritual world is vague, mystical and insubstantial. The real world is the world of the senses, of physical and material reality. If we can't see it, touch it, taste it, hear it or smell it, it must not be real, we think. But Lewis challenges us. "The Presence of God is the most real thing we ever encounter. If we are to have an appropriate image of God's presence, we should envision God's Presence as something *heavier* than matter."[3] God's presence is radiant like gold, heavy like lead, molten like lava. God's presence within us gives us radiance and substance of being.

Many ancients wrote of the majesty and beauty of God. Moses prayed, "Show me your glory" (Exodus 33:18). When we ask to be filled with the presence of the living God, we are asking to be filled with the majesty and beauty of Utter Reality.

We can't see the Presence, not because it's unreal or not there. We can't see it because the reality of the presence of God would blind us; it is on a wavelength and with a vibration beyond the capacity of our physical senses to receive. Why should this be so strange? Ultraviolet light is beyond the range of our senses. How much more is the wavelength of the very being of God. The range of wavelength and vibrations that we are able to receive through our eyes' receptors is actually quite limited. Why should it be strange to think that we might be surrounded by things and beings too beautiful to behold, too awesome to comprehend?

A rich world of miracle, majesty and terrible beauty underlies the Hebrew and Christian Scriptures. Lewis tried to restore that conception and experience of reality to us. As Leanne Payne says of him, "[C. S. Lewis] has enabled us to once again be 'at home' with *miracle, the native air* of the Scriptures and of the Spirit-enabled life."[4] Jesus was on intimate terms with this "archaic" world. Angels and devils, spirits in woodlands and water, the presence of Satan and the presence of God were all real to Jesus, not quaint notions of a superstitious, backward people. Why, Jesus even commanded a storm the way you and I might command an errant child, and the storm "obeyed" (Mark 4:39)!

No wonder we experience so little healing of the soul. We don't believe. Many in our day don't even believe we have a soul. And many more have lost all touch with the beautiful and terrible realities of the spiritual world. Our resources for healing the soul are paltry. But it need not be that way. We can recover the practice of God's presence and the reality of God's power to heal and to save.

When I began to take to heart Lewis's insights, my soul expanded. I felt as if I was taking in great drafts of fresh and verdant air blowing from a country I had never known but always longed for. My soul came *alive*. I'm not sure how else to say it. I started feasting on meat and mead for the soul. I felt satisfied. My mind had new ways to imagine the substance and beauty and heaviness of the Spirit of God. I had assumed the Holy Ghost was ghostly, insubstantial, intangible. Now I knew differently. God's Spirit is more real than flesh and blood, more invigorating than the first whiff of salt sea air on a windy day at the shore.

Of course we catch only glimpses of these realities of the Spirit. We are like blind persons who now and again see flashes of color. But when we do, when we catch a scent of the air that blows in from "the utter west" (Lewis's image of the kingdom of God), we are simultaneously satisfied and filled with unquenchable longing for the Real.

Over the years I have learned that the greatest gain from the healing of my own soul has not been relief from pain, though sometimes my pain has diminished. Nor has it been the end of all my struggles, though at many points I have been strengthened. Trial and temptation we have always with us, until Jesus comes again. The greatest gain has been the increase of my capacity to know, understand and love God. I have tasted what Paul prayed for in his words to the people of the Presence at Ephesus (slightly paraphrased to address it to us):

Christ can now dwell in our hearts through faith. And we, being rooted and grounded in love, now have power to comprehend with all the saints what is the breadth and length and height and depth of the love of Christ, and to know this love which surpasses knowledge, that we may be filled with all the fullness of God. (Ephesians 3:17-19)

The healing of the soul is for the setting of love in order. As I have beheld the breathtaking beauty and weightiness of the presence of God with me and within me, I have fallen in love—with my God. And that love, simply by being strengthened, helps reduce other loves, inordinate loves, to their appropriate sphere and influence. I feel more sound, more right, more solid at the center of my being. And I have discovered that becoming sound and solid all the way through was what I really wanted all along, much more than I wanted mere relief from pain.

Maybe you will discover the same joy in the Presence that has so delighted my own soul. But to do so, we need not only new images of the substance, weightiness and beauty of the presence of God. We need to cultivate a day-to-day *experience* of that presence.

FOR REFLECTION AND RESPONSE

1. What most strikes you about God's presence from this chapter? What was new for you?

2. What might help you grow in your conviction and experience of the reality of God's presence?

3. Write and speak out a prayer for God's presence and glory to fill you and for your eyes to be opened to the presence and love of God around you and within you.

5

Practicing God's Healing Presence

Sharon approached me one day during a meeting in our community. She needed prayer. She had just experienced a painful relational crash with a man, and it wasn't the first time. The two of them had started as friends, but she soon began to want to be more than friends. She cared deeply for him and asked for more friendship time. Feeling pressured, he withdrew. Sharon felt an immense sense of rejection and anger and was beginning to descend into depression. Having experienced a similar pattern in relationships with men several times before, she was losing hope and felt tempted to withdraw from all relationships.

I thanked her for having the courage to share her need with someone. I knew I was a safe person for her, because I was unavailable for a romantic relationship but could be caring and compassionate toward her.

I invited her to receive prayer at our next healing service. That evening God touched her heart, and as Sandra, another prayer minister, and I began to pray, we sensed that Sharon's relational pattern was rooted in her early relationship with her dad, who had been emotionally distant. She was choosing men who reminded her of her dad, pursuing them in the hope that the result would be different, but instead getting the same result again and again. Her hope was almost gone and her inner world almost shattered.

Where do you begin to pray when someone has such a deeply rooted set of hurts? We began with Sharon where I begin with anyone for whom I pray. We began to teach Sharon to practice God's healing presence and prepare herself to hear God's whispering voice. Sharon needed to begin to receive God's parental love and hear God's voice for herself. Until she had begun to take her eyes off herself and her pain and to focus on God's healing presence with her, she would have great difficulty seeing and overcoming her self-defeating ingrained patterns.

Sometimes in ministries of healing, people start to look to the prayer minister as their healer. But God is the one who brings healing. People need to learn to worship God, to see Jesus with the eyes of their heart, to hear his voice and to receive healing from him. So whenever I am called to help someone enter the healing journey, I begin by focusing on who God is. In fact, I rarely pray for people outside of environments in which there is strong, vital worship and a commitment to hear from God. Prayer outside of such a context is often very unproductive and unfocused.

We asked Sharon to picture Jesus with her, next to her. We asked her what she "saw" him doing or "heard" him saying. We encouraged her to enter in to the quiet worship song being led from the front. As she invited God's presence to be with her, her muscles started to relax, and her inner eye began to be lifted up to God and off her pain. She began to be able to hear and receive from God.

That day Sharon began to learn to practice God's presence and seek healing through worship. As she began to taste and see that the Lord is good, she gained strength to face her pain and receive truth and healing. She went on to experience deep healing for her soul and strength to make new choices.

Do you need prayer, or do you have opportunities to pray for others? Where will you begin? Begin with the practice of God's healing presence, just as Sharon did.

How do we encounter the presence of God? How do we cultivate an experience of God's real presence with us? If God's presence is so weighty and substantial, why do we so often experience God as distant and insubstantial? Why do we so often feel spiritually weightless?

A Failure of the Imagination

Here's my thesis: *We have immense difficulty practicing God's presence and keeping God's reality before our mind's eye because we have dismissed or denigrated our capacity to intuitively and imaginatively apprehend and encounter God.* We have lost the power of imagination and intuition. We have relegated all such knowledge to a subjective inner world. We have closed ourselves off from the unseen realities all around us. We have leveled out the world, demythologized it, turned it from poetry into prose. Our intuitions and our imagination have become capacities we distrust.

Of course this thesis is not mine alone. Many others have suggested a similar explanation for our paltry, tenuous experience of God's presence in our day.

Intuition is the capacity to grasp the whole, to see the pattern, to grasp the nature of a thing. Intuition is a capacity to perceive what we are examining, not in its details but as a whole cloth, as a tapestry weaving meaningful patterns out of interconnected threads.

Imagination is the capacity to picture something not present to our senses. It is our picture-making faculty.

These two capacities are different from each other, but they work together to help us apprehend things we can't see, either because the things are not before our eyes or because the things are supersensible, like God or angels or any spiritual being. Intuition is a receptor, like a radar dish. Imagination is a projector.

We are called to love God with our whole heart, our whole mind, our whole soul and our whole strength. Many of us have not yet learned to love God with our imagination and our intuition.

Throughout Scripture we are expected to encounter, know and love God through the imagination, in symbol, image and picture. In *Imagining God* Garrett Green notes that in Scripture God's revelation is almost always given first in the form of image and only afterward with explanatory words. "The imagination is the locus of revelation. It is the faculty through which revelation comes."[1]

Think about it. When God revealed himself, it was often through image, to the recipient's imaginative capacities. Think of Moses and the burning bush, Isaiah and the throne room of God, Ezekiel and the cherubim and seraphim, John and the son of man with burning eyes, white hair, glowing bronze feet and a voice like the sound of rushing waters in Revelation. Again and again in Scripture, God reveals himself through symbol and image, and then words are given to explain the image.

We often trust only words and so have lost the biblical pattern for God's self-revelation and our encounter with God. Having disregarded the imaginative and intuitive ways of knowing, we are surprised at how paltry our experience of God is.

Mystics and saints throughout the ages have taught about and cultivated the capacity to have a truly imaginative and intuitive experience that connects humans directly to unseen reality, to God, angels, demons. This dimension of intuition and imagination is the one Rudolf Otto talks about in his *Idea of the Holy*, when he speaks of "the numinous." Otto invites us to explore what people experienced when they encountered Jesus. Mark 10:32 captures it well: "And Jesus went before them: and they were amazed; and as they followed they were afraid" (KJV). The disciples and people experienced the numinous in

Jesus,[2] which made them afraid and amazed, but they also saw the rational and moral good in Jesus. In Jesus we both intuit God's presence and observe ethical goodness.

Otto suggests that the unique genius and beauty of Christian faith is the way rational and nonrational elements are jointly present in healthy and loving harmony.[3] He suggests that all of us, though not in equal measure, have the capacity to both intuit God's presence and rationally reflect on ideas of the goodness of God. This combination of goodness and numinous presence in loving harmony is at the heart of the Christian way.

MENTORED BY C. S. LEWIS

The first mentor to awaken my capacity to intuit and imagine unseen realities and let them influence my soul was C. S. Lewis. I went on a quest to read all of Lewis that I could, to let great drafts of good news blow through my mind as I entered a different mental landscape from the one I had inhabited up to that point. Coming into the thought world of Lewis was like visiting a foreign country. At first as I read Lewis, I focused primarily on his brilliantly logical thinking. But as I engaged with what he said about the imagination, his language was odd and difficult, his ideas strange. He spoke of the "weightiness" of spiritual realities. He wrote children's books and a space trilogy. He experienced having his mind "baptized" long before he became a Christian when he read *Phantastes* and *Lilith,* the fantasy works of George MacDonald. He spoke of his imaginative self as his deepest self. All this strangeness became the gateway into a new world of perception, intuition and imagination. His reasoning was sane and sound, but his ideas were surprising. I couldn't grasp them at first. But after patient reading and powerful corroborating experiences, I began to see.

I was like a blind man recovering his sight. At first the images I saw

were fuzzy and indistinct. The eyes of the heart that Paul puts such
emphasis on (see Ephesians 1:18-23) had been largely blind and certainly underdeveloped in me for many years. But now I began to see
with the eyes of my heart. I began truly to know, to intuit, God and
to trust what I was seeing and experiencing. I also now had words to
talk about earlier intuitions of God's real presence. But these capacities, long dormant, awakened slowly.

I must let you in on a secret now, and you may not like it. You may
feel I have pulled a "bait-and-switch" on you. You are reading a book
you thought promised healing. You thought that meant relief from
pain, the disappearance of nagging problems and addictive patterns.
I hope that by the end you get much of the help for which you hoped.
But now, this early in the book, you have come upon my greatest
hope for you. I want the eyes of your heart healed, that you might
"see" God, know God deeply, and find your Christian hope and in-
heritance made more real. I want you to grasp with all the saints how
deep and wide and high and ultimately incomprehensible is God's
love for you and all of us. That's the healing I most long for in your
life: the healing of your intuitive and imaginative capacities to know
God directly.

I am praying for you the prayers of Paul in his letter to the church
at Ephesus. Spend a few moments soaking in those prayers. You can
find them in Ephesians 1:17-23 (especially vv. 17-18) and 3:14-21.
Paul prays for us to enter into profound encounter with God. I want
your head and your heart brought together in this unity and synergy
of intimate connection with God. This intimacy is the foundation for
all divine healing.

The ministry of healing holds many dangers when spiritual power
becomes the focus. We are to be Presence-centered—oriented on intimacy with God—more than power-centered. Above all we are to be
Person-centered. It is all about an intimate love relationship with

God. It is all about Jesus. As we come to know the God with whom we have become one, the healing power of God's presence within us is released to transform us.

THE SPLIT BETWEEN THE HEAD AND HEART

How were our intuitive and imaginative capacities to know God shriveled and debilitated? Leanne Payne suggests an answer to this question by contrasting two ways of knowing: "Head and heart symbolize the two ways of knowing: the discursive reason on the one hand, and the intuitive, symbolic, feeling ways of knowing that have to do with faith and love, prayer, worship, the sacraments, and repentance on the other."[4] A fundamental disagreement occurred between Plato and Aristotle in regard to head and heart. Plato embraced intuitive ways of knowing, while Aristotle did not.

> Aristotle thought experience (observation) and reason together were capable alone of putting men in touch with the real. He rejected Plato's other way of knowing, which included divine inspiration, poetic awe, prophetic insight, and the way of love, the way of picture, metaphor, myth, symbol, and communion. Imagination and intuition provide the material for the creative idea. The rational powers bring to bear a shaping critique. What a wondrous thing to have the Rules and the Pictures not at war.[5]

The split between head and heart, between analytical reason and intuitive imagination, reached a crucial fork in the road in the thinking of Immanuel Kant. Kant decided that all interpretive activity of the mind, all attempts to comprehend the world out there, tell us more about the structures of the mind than about the nature of the world. He discounted human beings' capacity to know anything about the unseen world or metaphysical reality through intuition. In the Western world, we have all followed in Kant's footsteps. We do not trust our intuition and imagination as means of gaining information about objective reality. Is it any wonder that our capacity to know God through communion with God, our ability to sense and cultivate a direct experience of God's presence, is so stunted and starved?

Having said this, I want to add a caution. When we set our mind toward God, God's real presence is with us whether or not we sense or experience it. We sense God's presence at times; at other times we don't. What's more, our temperament, how intuitive and imaginative we are, affects how strongly we "feel" the presence of God. As a fairly intuitive person, I rarely lose entirely my sense of connection to God, my awareness of his presence. Other people are very rational or very oriented to sensory data and don't "feel" God's presence nearly as often or as intensely. The point is our mindset, not the intensity of our experiences, which will depend on many factors.

Here I must also confront a virus common to healing ministries that will be examined and diagnosed later at more length. Some healing ministries value intuitive and imaginative capacities more than rational capacities and create a hierarchy of worth based on the intensity and frequency of a person's spiritual experiences. Nothing could be more antithetical to healing than this attitude. It is an elitism that sees primarily rational or sensory people as less close to God and less valuable for God's work in the world. People who know God largely through their rational faculties are treated as second-class citizens of God's kingdom by the more intuitive, and vice versa.

Scripture paints a very different picture of the way God assigns value and worth—for example, see 1 Corinthians 12. Among God's people we need the effective exercise of each person's primary strengths and capacities. I will help you with the imaginative and intuitive side of things, and you will help me keep my feet on the ground and my head screwed on straight. Both of us are equally valuable. In fact, some of the functions we value the least are given particular honor in God's estimation. So whenever we catch a whiff of elitism, let's quickly clear the air!

One of the most powerful prayer groups I was ever part of was a threesome. We were African American, Latino and white. Each time we prayed, we heard God in ways distinctive to our temperament. Brenda Salter McNeil often had sensory impressions, I had intuitive nudges, and Pedro Aviles always thought of relevant Scriptures. Each of us in our unique way contributed to what God wanted to say to us and minister in and through us. It was a joy to be set free to know and hear God in our personal uniqueness and to give our gifts to one another.

I challenge you, then, to recognize that our culture and our training have taught us not even to expect that we can make contact with external spiritual reality through intuition and imagination. I am recovering these capacities, and I encourage you to seek them as well. You may not focus on them to the degree that I do. But it is essential for you to welcome whatever intuitive and imaginative capacities you do have into the mix of the ways you seek to know and love God. To be "surprised by joy," as Lewis often said, is to connect directly with the Source of joy.

STEPS INTO THE PRESENCE OF GOD

So how do we cultivate our intuitive and imaginative capacities to know God's real presence? How do we tune our receptors (intuition) and capture good images for our mind's projector (imagination)?

When I decided to follow God, I assumed God would speak only through my reading the Bible or hearing someone teach from the Bible. That's what I was taught. I was taught to distrust my feelings and intuitions. After all, feelings and intuitions are quite changeable and can be influenced by what I had for dinner or someone's funny look or offhand comment. And only the Bible claims to be God's unique Word for humankind.

So I read the Bible, and I found that it did ring true, brought needed wisdom and perspective, and helped me know and grow closer to God. Reading the Bible built up my knowledge of Jesus and provided a rich stock of biblical images from which to draw. But the Bible gave me principles and examples of God's *general* will. I came to a point where I wanted more. I wanted to know God's specific desires for me, for my life and for the lives of others I cared about. I wanted to walk in closer intimacy with God and work in closer partnership with God.

The first step for those who want to sanctify and strengthen their intuitive and imaginative capacities is to immerse themselves in Scripture. As we become familiar with the written Word, we come closer to breathing the air that the people in Scripture breathed, people who heard directly from God and who have provided a wealth of images that picture who God is and what God says when he speaks. But ultimately we want to encounter the same God those people encountered and to know him intuitively and imaginatively for ourselves.

Let me challenge you, then, to learn to hear God as you fill your mind and heart with the Scriptures. That step is always first, foremost and foundational. The problem for me was that I had been taught that hearing God generally from Scripture was valuable but that hearing God more specifically was *not* valuable or necessary.

I will never forget when I was first challenged to seek greater intimacy with God and learn to hear his voice and sense his real presence. I was a college student, committed to Christ, serving Jesus in some tangible ways. But my intimacy with God was unsatisfying, while some Christians I knew had a closeness to God that I found challenging and even a little intimidating. They seemed to know God, and they claimed they had words and nudges from God's Spirit that made a difference in the lives of others. I longed for a closer connection to God, but I feared it too.

Then I read a book by Rosalind Rinker that defined prayer as a dialogue between two people who love each other.[6] Her statement was so simple, but it really helped me because I had assumed hearing from God was complicated, beyond my reach, requiring a certain kind of "spiritual" personality.

Rinker challenged readers to picture the eyes of Jesus when they prayed. Some people of faith believe that creating or using any picture of Jesus, whether painted or imagined, is idolatry, the worship of an image rather than of God himself. For them, imagining Jesus in our mind's eye violates the Second Commandment (to make no graven images of God). Rinker argued that such people have entirely missed the point of that commandment. The commandment was not intended to shut down our imagination in prayer but only to keep us from turning the products of our imagination into the focus of our worship. In laying down this commandment God was fighting an essential confusion in the human heart: our tendency to worship the images themselves rather than let them point to the One that is beyond them, giving focus and feeling to our worship.

I will never forget the July day I went for a walk in a local park. First I focused on and began to feel present to my surroundings. I listened to the chattering brook, I noticed the brilliant green of the leaves and the bright blue of the sky. I watched a cloud meander across the horizon. Then I affirmed in prayer that God was with me and within me, thanking him for his presence. With eyes open, I pictured Jesus' eyes, full of compassion and wisdom, looking at me with an expectant, waiting gaze. I'm not sure how else to describe the "sense" I had of his presence and his look. I rested in that gaze for several minutes. Then, with the beauty of the park in the background, I began to ask this very present Jesus questions that were on my heart, and he began to answer.

When I began to understand and embrace the crucial place of my imagination in worshiping and listening to God, my relationship with God underwent a quantum leap forward. From then on when I prayed, I pictured the eyes of Jesus. I spoke right to Jesus, imagining that he was present with me (because of course he was!). My dialogue with God took on an immediacy and interactivity that I had never experienced before and would never live without again. Such a simple step—and with such a profound impact!

Have you taken that simple step? Could you?

JESUS THE LORD . . . OF OUR IMAGINATION

We can create environments that contain biblical and Christian images to help focus and free our worship. The cross, the altar, images of shepherds and sheep, pictures of the wounded healer Jesus touching the hurting, scenes of the accused and convicted Jesus proclaiming the release of captives—all can help our mind and heart tune in to the being and nature of the incarnate God. Scenes of clouds hovering darkly, with lightning bolts and implied turbulent rumblings, point to the mystery and majesty of the God who is beyond all human images and metaphors.

In worship your mind will focus on something. If your worship environment is imagery-impoverished and barren of beauty, your mind will wander into daydreams, images that may interrupt or derail your worship. You will look at the attractive guy or pretty woman across the aisle or replay in your mind the movie you watched last night. We human beings are incurably and wonderfully visual and imaginative. Our imagination and intuition will be driven toward meaningful worship or will drift into meaningless meandering. God has made us this way. If you do not feed your heart with nourishing images of the good, the true, the beautiful and the holy, you will let it be inhabited by images that feed the crooked, the deceptive, the self-serving and the lustful. No other option is open.

Jesus needs to be Lord of our imagination! Our imagination needs cleansing and sanctification. We need a restoration of the holy imagination that the mystics and prophets throughout the ages have understood and cultivated.

Admiration of beauty and virtue is good for the soul (see Philippians 4:8). Through our intuitive receptors and imaginative projector, we take into ourselves whatever we fix our gaze upon and admire. The eye is the lamp of the body, Jesus said. What we look at determines how much light enters into our inner being. Visual images that point us toward what is unseen cooperate to elicit true and meaningful worship.

Lewis describes the effort required to learn this practice of the presence of God and also the result that unfolds as we learn:

> The real problem of the Christian life comes where people do not usually look for it. It comes the very moment you wake up each morning. All your wishes and hopes for the day rush at you like wild animals. And the first job each morning consists in shoving them all back; in listening to that other voice, taking that other point of view, letting that other larger, stronger, quieter life come flowing in. . . .
>
> We can do it only for moments at first. But from those moments the new sort of life will be spreading through our systems because now we are letting him work at the right part of us.[7]

At first it is very difficult to fix our mind on God and his healing presence, to set the eyes of our heart to see and the ears of our soul to hear what God wants of us. But after a while it becomes easier, so that only a gentle pressure need be applied to our will to pay attention to God's Spirit. This is the practice of the presence that has been emphasized by the saints throughout the ages. Images and symbols, natural and Christian, are key catalysts for this crucial practice.

Such intimacy with God is not beyond us but within our reach as we depend on the Spirit to provide us with strength and capacity to find and hear and obey God. And this practice opens up a secure and sacred environment in which God can do healing work. Practicing God's presence is like an artist's canvas: by itself it is not the painting. But without the canvas, the painting will never begin.

FOR REFLECTION AND RESPONSE

1. What environments most help you to worship God?

2. What symbols and experiences most help you connect to God?

3. What has helped you in the past to cultivate your imaginative capacities to know God?

4. What do you want to do next to cultivate those capacities?

6

Hearing God's Whisper

I often have a sense that God is whispering to my heart. One crucial moment in my listening and healing journey happened when I was praying about this very book in my favorite place to walk, the beautiful gardens of Cantigny, west of Chicago. I had walked through the gardens, around the McCormick mansion, and come to the monument where Robert and Amy McCormick are buried. I sat on a bench, looked up to heaven in my spirit and asked God what he wanted me to do with this healing book. Should I write it? What should it be on? Who should it be for?

My heart was receptive. The beauty of the gardens had tuned my soul to silence and opened my heart to the whispering voice of God. I sensed Jesus' presence, and I had a strong impression that he was speaking right to my soul.

He invited me to come walking in the gardens of the soul throughout the fall season that had just begun. He promised to walk beside me, to sit next to me on this very bench in the shadow of Amy McCormick, who loved music and beauty, and to have some conversations about the art of healing the soul.

God made it clear that I needed to write this book first for my own soul and that our conversations would bring wisdom and perspective regarding the healing journey of my own life. When I asked if I was writing for others as well, I felt only a silence from God's Spirit. I wasn't to know that yet. I was to live in loving dialogue with God for this season and to write the book that my own soul most needed.

What a precious moment that was. God nudged me to write a book that would be very personal and autobiographical, because I would write it first for my own healing journey. A sense of the presence and heaviness of God's Spirit weighed on me over the next several days, deepening and clarifying the invitation to walk in the garden of the soul with Jesus. Sometimes I started to daydream about writing a book on healing that would touch many other hearts, but as soon as I did, the clarity and peacefulness of God's presence and call would dissipate. The dream of future influence undermined the purpose of God's invitation to me. I was to let God worry about the future while I pursued the goal God had given me: to let his Spirit influence my soul as we had conversation together.

Silence and inner stillness were the medium in which God's whispers rang out in my soul, the way a small clear bell resounds in a quiet courtyard.

As we walk the healing journey, no other single thing we can do may have greater impact than learning to listen to God. God's voice is the healing voice, just as God's presence is the healing presence. We must hear the voice of God reverberate in our soul, exposing the lies about our unlovability, worthlessness or despair and speaking the truth. We must.

But the practice of listening to God can be fraught with confusion and misunderstanding. In this chapter we will explore how we can learn to listen to God, hear his whispering voice and distinguish it from confusing influences. This practice will have immense implications for the healing journey and will enrich our whole life.

Our physical and relational worlds constantly demand attention. Voices from those arenas scream at us incessantly. But the spiritual world *whispers*. To hear the whispering voice of God, we must get quiet, be alone and let silence deepen into words. That's what happened to me in those few autumn days at Cantigny. What you hold in your hand grew out of those moments of hearing God speak.

How do you hear God speak? How do you practice living with a constant consciousness that God is with you and wants to speak? How do you hear the healing voice of God whisper truth to your hurting soul? How do you hear God speak to your heart so you can minister to the hearts of others?

Of course, how you listen and how I listen will be different. I think of my friend Sandy. Sandy grew up in the Christian Reformed Church and was given a wonderful theological and Christian foundation. She once told me she doesn't have a charismatic bone in her body. We have spent hours arguing about the practice of listening to God and the diverse ways in which God speaks. She taught me a lot about how God will speak to each of us according to our temperament.

But as Sandy and I got beyond the surface in our discussion, we both recognized the many ways that God speaks to her. She is as committed to hearing God's voice and direction in her life as I am. But we have different ways of talking about listening prayer.

As I have spent time with people in a great diversity of Christian traditions, I have seen that we all are longing for and seeking to hear the voice of God, first in Scripture but also very personally. We have different ways of describing and pursuing the practice, but we all seek to hear from God and respond to God's whispers and nudges.

GROWING IN INTIMACY AND WISDOM

In the last chapter I recounted my first faltering steps into the substantial and radiant spiritual reality of God's healing presence. As I began the journey, I experienced several benefits of learning to listen to God.

First and most important, my intimacy with God grew, as did my sense of God's reality. This result, after all, is the main point, isn't it? Dallas Willard poses a telling question: "What kind of relationship is it where there are not specific communications?"[1] Then he makes this point:

> To the individual believer, who is, by the very fact of relationship to Christ, indwelt by the Holy Spirit of God, there is granted to us as needed the direct impression of the Spirit of God on our spirit, imparting the knowledge of God's will in matters of the smallest and greatest importance. This guidance has to be sought and waited for. We ask and keep on asking.[2]

The second benefit of hearing God's voice: I gained wisdom and perspective regarding choices I had to make, including how to pursue healing and how to minister it to others. God is, after all, the smartest Person in the universe.

Sometimes God's wisdom comes as very specific direction for the choices I face or the people I pray for face. Years ago when I was praying about whether to go into campus ministry or to become an engineer at Exxon, I went for a long walk in the hills of County Tipperary, Ireland, where I was spending the summer. I heard God say, not audibly but almost, "Go back to the States, spend a year at Exxon as an engineer, and then enter campus ministry."

Whoa! That was clear. And it's just what I did. It turned out well.

A couple of years later, when I faced the decision of whether to marry MaryKay Demet, a coworker in campus ministry, I went for a walk on the streets of Madison, Wisconsin. I looked up to the heavens and cried out the uncertainty in my soul. Again, not audibly but almost, I heard God clearly respond. This time God said, "It's your choice!"

I wanted to say, "Can I have that one again?" I didn't want God to tell me it was my choice. I wanted God to tell me it was his will, so I could be secure in the decision.

That day I had to grow up a little. God didn't want me to be childishly dependent. God wanted me to become a mature decision-maker. It was right for me to ask, but it was also right for God to throw the ball back in my court.

Many people are looking for God to make every little decision for them. Some go as far as to say they ask God which color of socks to put on each day. The belief that God is involved in our daily life is admirable, but such immature dependency is not. Imagine a person going through life depending on someone else to tell him what color of socks to put on. Such a person would barely move beyond the developmental stage of early infancy.

God longs for partners and companions, people who will grow into a relationship of love and mutuality with him. Of course God will always be far up the ladder of being from us. But he wants us to grow and expand all that we are able. He is looking for maturity and mutuality.

At the same time, God did give me real wisdom the night I asked him about my marriage decision. That evening God gave me a strong sense of his presence and the impression that he would bless whatever decision I made. It would really be okay to go for it, or it would really be okay to seek another partner instead. The one "word" I heard from God was that if I were to marry MaryKay, I would become much more of a servant. That's probably true of *any* successful marriage, though in retrospect I can see how MaryKay has been especially helpful to me in that way! (Yes, I did choose to marry MaryKay, and we continue to journey together some twenty-five years later. You would have to ask her if I've become a better servant. Honestly though, from then to now, the only direction for me in servanthood was up.)

Sometimes the wisdom we get as we listen to God doesn't make our decision but only puts our decision in perspective. That's often just as valuable.

The principles about listening to God for direction also apply to listening to God for healing for ourselves and others. We are not trying to "fix" people but collaborating with God to lead them toward maturity. We do not aim for immature dependency on a prayer minister or an oft-repeated healing experience. We want others to become mature, hearing from God for themselves.

This points to another danger to avoid in the ministry of healing. Sometimes as prayer ministers we create dependency on us; or if we are seeking healing, we become dependent on some prayer minister because we don't think we can hear God for ourselves. The tendency toward dependency is one of the greatest dangers in the healing ministry and the spiritual life.

Our role is to point people to Jesus. Our goal is to look to Jesus. But our ego needs get involved all too readily. Many prayer ministers feel an intense pressure to perform when they pray for others. And many people seeking healing are looking for a special prayer minister who will provide them with a spiritual charge. These performance and dependency temptations can be the biggest derailers of ministries of healing.

We begin well, but then our performance or the experience becomes the focus and our neediness gets in the way. Healing ministries tend to draw needy people, both seeking prayer and offering prayer. We needy people are often aware of how deeply we need healing. But neediness can become a catalyst for all kinds of confusion as we try too hard to perform, look too much to a particular person or become dependent on a particular experience.

The point is Jesus! Not our performance. Not our experience at any particular moment. Just Jesus. And Jesus can bring perspective any time we find our heart confused.

Whenever I am lost in an inner world of painful self-doubt and accusation, or locked in dynamics of insecurity and neediness, I seek to get quiet, to really slow the inner chatter and hear a healing word from God. I seek to unhook, let go and get out of my inner world, becoming present to God and the world around me. Then I am more able to hear his voice. What God says in those moments is always a wise word, giving perspective on God's work and my identity. I believe God is often whispering a wise and healing word to our heart, could we but learn to hear and embrace it.

PRAYING FOR IMPACT

Third, learning to hear God has increased my impact on the lives of others. I have become a better partner with God, especially in the ministry of healing prayer. How could it be any different?

Here's an example from the ministry of intercession: In my early Christian life, my prayers for others consisted of requests for whatever I thought they needed. When I first began to look into the eyes of Jesus and stopped my running monologue in prayer, God was finally able to get a word in edgewise. Paul tells us that Jesus is at God's right hand, interceding for you and me (Romans 8:34)—so I would ask Jesus how he was praying for the people I cared about. For example, I asked Jesus what he most wanted for my friend Bruce, what he was praying for Bruce's life. Immediately I felt a nudge to turn to Philippians 2, which calls us to be like Jesus, who didn't think of himself first but was a servant to all.

I began to pray Philippians 2 for Bruce every day. He was two thousand miles away in Los Angeles, and I had not been in touch with him for a while. Three weeks to the day after I had begun praying Philippians 2 for Bruce, I got a letter from him. He wrote:

> I can't seem to get out of Philippians 2 in my Bible reading. Every
> day God seems to be showing me something else about how to
> serve others, and especially my wife and my family. What's
> more, my wife is challenging me with lots of ideas these days
> about how I can be a better servant. So I guess that's how you
> can pray for me.

Ha! I was already on the case! I can't tell you what it did for my
faith and practice of listening prayer to experience such a concrete
example of how to enter into what Jesus was already praying for another's life.

I don't often receive such specific direction, but I often get insight
into how God is at work in the lives of my friends and how I can best
collaborate with God in prayer. In that sense I am entering into the
prayer life of Jesus for my friends. After all, I am in union with Jesus.
The more my praying and living arise out of that union, the more
powerful and profound will be my experience and awareness of seeing lives change.

I now ask the very same question I asked about Bruce whenever I
am seeking healing or ministering healing through prayer. "Jesus,
how are you praying for me?" Or, "How are you praying for this sufferer who has come to me seeking your healing presence?"

Don't you long for a clear change in the lives of others when you
pray with and for them? Of course, it's not our prayers that change
people's lives; God does that. But the God who changes people's lives
invites us to be part of his activity through prayer. We enter into his
prayer and his work when we ask *how* he is praying and working.
Then our prayers give God opportunity to deepen and expand his
work in a person's life.

The goal of collaborating with God even affects *how* I pray and what I do with my eyes, hands and body as I pray for others. When I ask Jesus how he is praying for sufferers who have come to me, I often get an image of Jesus with his hand on their heart, praying for its healing. Or if I sense Jesus might be commissioning them for ministry, I may see his hands on their head. I then do what I see or sense Jesus doing: I place my hand over their heart or on their head.

Of course I must practice discernment and care in the ways I touch people as I pray for them. If I am praying for a woman, I always ask if it is all right for me to lay hands on her. I generally ask men as well, but I have found that women who may have experienced abuse especially need to be asked. When I see Jesus healing a woman's heart, I ask her to cross her hands on her chest, and then I place my hand on her hands.

A prayer minister I know just prayed yesterday for a person who was feeling called to evangelism. My friend got down on her knees, placed her hands on the person's feet and prayed Isaiah 52:7: "How beautiful . . . are the feet of those who bring good news."

Often the Spirit of God will confirm what Jesus is praying for people, sometimes even with sensations. People called to speak the Word of God may feel their lips burn or their heart burn within them, and people called to evangelism may feel their feet tingle. So when I pray I often keep my eyes open, listening for what God may be saying and watching for how the person is responding. Throughout, I seek to listen to God's whispering voice and gentle nudges.

ASKING GOD QUESTIONS

How can you learn to listen to God? The heart of the practice is learning to recognize that God is concretely present with you and then to ask good questions of this very present God. Then wait until he speaks into your heart and mind.

When I pray, first I focus my mind on God's presence by looking into the eyes of Jesus or looking around at nature and up to the heavens, opening my soul to God. Sometimes I focus on a biblical or Christian image that jumpstarts my intuitive and imaginative capacities. If speaking in tongues is part of your Christian experience, you may find it helpful too. It quickly helps many to tune in to God not just with their rational minds but also with their intuitive receptors.

Then I regularly ask God more general questions.

What are you saying? What are you saying to me? I often ask this question to discern what God wants me to do next for my character growth, in my ministry and in my relationships with others. God often wants to whisper to us about these three areas. But I also ask this question in relation to healing, for myself and for others.

What are you doing? What can I do with you? I often ask this question as I am praying for another and wondering what to focus on. The person may have brought me many needs, but God often wants to minister to just one at a time. I also ask this question when I am trying to choose where to focus ministry time and energy. I want to catch the wave of what God is doing, not just ask God to bless what I want to do.

What are you praying? How can I enter into your prayers for this person or this situation? As I mentioned earlier, sometimes I ask Jesus to show me not only *what* he is praying but *how* he is praying. Is he praying for the healing of this person's heart, or their commissioning to ministry, or something else?

What's the one thing you want to minister to during this prayer time?
What's the one next step you want this person to take?

We can feel overwhelmed by the needs people share with us and by our own needs as well. The above questions can help us focus. Focusing on how Jesus is praying and what one thing Jesus might want to do or work on helps immensely. It breaks the healing journey down to just the next step.

These questions also help us defuse the pressure to perform in prayer, whether by being healed right now or by ministering healing to a suffering soul who has come to us. We can feel inadequate and afraid that God won't heal us, or use us, or speak through us. Healing is the work of God, but we get to partner with God in taking that next step. We are collaborators with God and can relax and let God nudge us toward what we are to receive or minister. The healing journey, though sometimes dramatic, is always incremental. We just need to take the next step.

Whether I am practicing God's presence and listening for God's voice is a good litmus test of my spiritual health. When I start to feel out of touch with God, I usually must acknowledge that I have neglected these two things: focusing on God's real presence and asking God's Spirit good questions.

When I am in a vicious cycle of obsessive thinking about some struggle, hurt, insult, failure, fear or disappointment, I need help to listen to God and hear his voice. I am unable to focus on God's presence with me or hear God speak when I am in a lot of pain. At those moments I need to talk it out to somebody safe who will accept me readily. Or I need to walk in a forest preserve until I have unhooked and relaxed inside and let go of the mental reruns. I need to become truly present to my surroundings and to my God. Patterns of circular and painful thinking are blocks to becoming present to God and hearing his whispering voice. Many people have told me they have the same need to unhook from any vicious cycle of anxious thinking if they are to hear from God.

Constant noise and activity can be a serious barrier to hearing God speak. Some find it very difficult to be companionably alone with themselves and God. Silence and solitude can be uncomfortable, even frightening. A spiritual mentor or guide can help us get quiet, deal with our fears and anxious inner voices, and then begin to listen for God's whispers.

Doug and Marilyn Stewart are good friends of mine who have led many neophytes into their first experiences of silent retreats and listening to God. They note that often people are frightened of silence. We tend to fill up our life and being with noise and distraction, because we are afraid of what might happen if we got truly quiet. We might face pain that we've been stuffing down. Or we might experience nothing and feel we have failed, proved inadequate once again. Still, we will rarely hear from God without getting quiet. Thus many of us need a guide, mentor or retreat leader to help us take the first steps and interpret our experience.

IS THAT YOU, GOD?

How do we know when it's God and not just our own heart or a stray thought or wishful thinking? We can't know for sure. In fact, in my experience when people become convinced that they can always tell when it's God, they become dangerous. None of us is beyond self-deception. We are all capable of confusing the whispering voice of our own heart with the whispering voice of God's Spirit.

But it's a very good thing to hear our own heart. That's often our first step.

I have learned to ask myself certain questions that help me know immediately that a word is from my own heart and not from God. When I hear a whisper or have an intuition of some "word" that is related to very strong needs I have, I am most likely hearing my own heart, however powerful the experience and however much I want to believe I am hearing God's voice. A friend who teaches people to learn to listen to God likes to say, "Beware of the three Gs: gold, glory and a particular guy or gal. Whenever a 'word' relates to any of the three Gs, treat it with caution and skepticism."

Once a man prayed for me and saw pictures of stadiums overflowing with people in response to my ministry. *Beware!* I told my soul.

That's a "glory" word. That appeals to grandiosity, a particular liability for ambitious men. Fortunately, I'm aware that I have strong desires to feel special and important. It's best to deflate the "stadium pictures": *Wouldn't that be nice? Don't count on it! Don't even think about it! It's not good for the health of your soul.*

Some people get a "word" about a person they "should" marry. That's one of the three Gs: a particular guy or gal. Don't pay any attention to the "word." Just build the relationship. Don't bring God in as the great tiebreaker in the sky. Give God space to tell the other person too. You will avoid much heartache if you hold very loosely any word about marrying some particular person, especially when you've just met her or him.

Other people want hearing from God to be almost like opening a fortune cookie. "You will meet someone new this week." "Your fortunes are looking up." "You will have a great financial opportunity shortly." Hearing God is *not* like opening a fortune cookie. It is not magic to be manipulated: God is "not a tame lion," as C. S. Lewis puts it. God does not exist to revolve around us. God is there to be worshiped, loved, followed and obeyed. Hearing God does not tame God to our wishes but rather often tames our wishes to God's.

You must learn to hear God through personal experience and experimentation. There is no good way to learn but by trying! By analogy, animals learn their master's voice, children learn their parents' voices, and a lover learns his companion's voice, so that it becomes dear, reverberates in the soul, communicates the person's presence. How do you recognize the voice of your beloved (if you have one) when you answer the phone? By experience, by the timbre and the quality of the voice, and by the presence that is communicated along with that voice. When I'm away from my wife, MaryKay, my heart leaps when I pick up the phone and hear her rich, warm, mahogany voice. I have no doubt who it is! And with her voice I can feel her presence. So it is with God as we grow in listening prayer.

I look for the following qualities as signs of the experience of hearing God: the unexpectedness of a specific message, its weight of authority, a spirit of peace attending it and conformity of the content to what I know Jesus to be like. These signals give me great assurance in day-to-day life with Christ as companion and colaborer. Can I still be wrong in believing I have heard from God? Of course. But probably not often if I am consistently attuned to an ongoing conversation with God.

It is hard at first. When I was first learning to hear God, it was like coming out of a fog. Our materialistic, technology-oriented world had trained me to distrust my feelings and intuitions and to doubt the reality of things I cannot see. Of course it was not easy to hear a Person who is physically inaudible and visually intangible. What's more, the constant noise of our wordy world crowds out the gentle whispers of the Spirit. I have found that too much television blurs the vision of the eyes of the heart. Somehow television exercises a controlling influence on our imagination and dulls our openness to unseen reality. Television puts us into a passive mode, giving control to the programmer. Listening to God involves an engaged, active imagination, not limited to what can be known through the senses.

Our therapeutic culture trains us to listen endlessly to our own feelings. We are fascinated by the inner world of our chattering selves. But the practice of listening prayer is fundamentally different from tuning in to the anxious or painful or pleasurable feelings and voices within. Rarely can we come into silence without first recognizing and hearing the inner chatter. But we must turn away from that endless inner noise to become truly quiet and receptive to the whispers of God.

Listening prayer always involves looking outward. We tune our mind's eye and ear to a real presence that is outside of us, even when it speaks from within us. Here is why I look for an *unexpected* quality of a whispered word as a sign of God's voice. When I get an image or an intuition of what to pray for and simultaneously experience a small jolt of surprise—*I didn't expect to hear that!*—I am encouraged. I may well be hearing from another Person and not just from myself.

THE LISTENING-TO-GOD LEARNING CURVE

During a conference in which I was learning to listen to God while I served on the prayer team, a man and I were praying for another young man. As I asked Jesus what he was doing and wanted to do in prayer, I saw the word *pornography* spelled out. I didn't know how it applied and was afraid to ask! But I took a risk: I asked if the issue of pornography was something God might want us to pray for. The young man replied, "Not really." I said, "Hey, I'm new at this listening to God thing. I probably just got it wrong." So the other man and I prayed for areas in which the young man did need healing.

At the end of our prayers, I walked away. I had made it about half-way across the ballroom floor where we were holding the conference, when the man who had been my prayer coworker practically tackled me. He said, "That word was for me, not for the guy for whom we were praying. I came a thousand miles to this conference to deal with my addiction to pornography, and I hadn't worked up the guts to tell anyone. I am leaving tomorrow, and if you hadn't said what you said, I would have left without ever dealing with it."

He and I then went into an absolutely beautiful time of prayer for cleansing and coming free. Afterward I counseled him about practical steps he needed to take to settle into real change.

I had the right word, but I had the wrong guy! That's what it's like when we begin. It is like coming out of a mental fog. Our souls have been tainted by doubt and unbelief about all things unseen and spiritual. But don't let the difficulty deter you from learning to hear from

God! No other practice is so rewarding, so meaningful and so lifelong in its impact, and not just for the healing journey.

FINAL WORDS OF ENCOURAGEMENT

To round out the chapter, I offer a couple of encouragements. First, don't let your expectations of what it feels like to hear from God, or even what I have shared from my experience, keep you from hearing God in the special ways that fit your temperament and wiring. As I have mentioned, my rational friends tend to hear God through ideas and study of Scripture. My artistic friends tend to see images or have kinesthetic (touch) experiences (like gardening) that help them hear from God. My nature-oriented friends love to connect to God through the great outdoors. God is big enough to speak to you in the ways that fit your temperament.

Second, don't listen to the unbelief in your soul that would destroy experiences with God and the whisper of God almost the moment they come. Reject those blanket doubts. One day as my friend Jose and I were praying together, God overwhelmed both of us with incredible pictures of his love for Jose and his healing presence. We finished. Within one minute of our "Amen," Jose was wondering whether anything we had thought God had said was valid. Did God say it? How can we hear from God anyway? Within five minutes Jose had completely deconstructed all the good he had received from listening to God.

It turned out that Jose was wracked with anxiety and doubt because of a painful upbringing. He needed a mother! Having never learned to receive love and nurture, he immediately questioned any experience of love, whether from God or from other people. His education in an elite college had also taught him to doubt the reality of anything unseen and to turn a critical gaze on all experiences before he had even finished experiencing them.

Leanne Payne calls the tendency to immediately turn a critical, skeptical eye on imaginative and intuitive experience "the disease of introspection." She challenges people to repent of and renounce this sinful and diseased habit of mind if they ever want to come into contact with the real presence of God and the healing whispers of God's voice.

Our whole culture needs to confess and renounce its unbelief in anything unseen, its radical doubt about imaginative and intuitive experience and knowledge. We need to relearn that nurturing, responsive union with Another in which communication takes place even if audible words are not spoken. We need to let spiritual experiences have their way with us before we turn our hypercritical gaze upon them.

Often when I have sensed that God has communicated directly to me, I will write down the message in a prayer journal and just let it sit for several days. I find that when it is a word, nudge or impression from God, letting it sit and giving it time leads to a growing sense of its rightness and an increasing intensity of its impact. Ignatius of Loyola called this sense of growing peace "consolation." If, on the other hand, the impression dissipates or the word has a superficial or even negative impact, then I conclude it was a word from my own heart or from some other spirit. Ignatius called this process "desolation."

I will often share those words that deepen with close friends, testing them with people who know and love me. And remember, it's always good to know what our own heart wants. So if I have heard a word from my own heart, I pat myself on the heart and tell myself, *I hear you, little guy.*

Finally, God is greater than our ability or inability to hear him. You are not doomed to a life of failure or futility if you are not yet good at hearing God's whispering voice. Wherever there is a consistent desire to hear God's voice and respond, God's whispering voice will become progressively clearer. That healing voice is speaking even now. Can you hear? Will you listen?

FOR REFLECTION AND RESPONSE

1. Reflect on any experiences you have had of being nudged by God or getting an impression of what God wanted you to do or pray for. What do you learn from your own experiences?

2. What might help you grow in learning to listen to God?

3. Spend some time now asking God the questions that are on your heart. Listen for God's whispering voice to respond. Write out whatever you sense. You may want to begin a journal in which you keep a record of what you sense God might be saying to you.

7

Understanding Gender Identity

John came to me for prayer during one of our Wednesday healing services. He was in his early twenties. That service had focused on healing in areas of gender and sexuality, and with John I expected to pray for some sexual addiction or struggle, as I often have for men. But as he began to talk with me, I realized his struggle was very different from those of most men I had prayed with before. He hated himself as a man and had almost destroyed his sexual drive through repression and fear.

John's father was very authoritarian and had belittled John harshly. John's image of masculinity involved violence and sarcasm. He had never experienced male affirmation, and his soul was starving. In addition, he had been taught in his church about the dangers and temptations of his sex drive, but he had never been taught to see the sex drive as a good gift from God that merely needed to be channeled rightly.

John's distorted image of masculinity and his fear of the power of his own sexuality combined to turn him against himself. He had emotionally self-emasculated. He had lost the capacity to be aroused and to affirm his sexual nature.

Up to then I had rarely prayed with men for the recovery of a healthy drive for sex. I have since often prayed for such men. Especially in the church, we don't know how to teach people to embrace their gender identity and sexuality. We have often failed to distinguish between self-control and self-hatred.

John's struggle involved his rejection of himself as a man, and at the heart of that self-rejection were very distorted images of men. After I invited John to practice God's presence and listen for God's voice, I began to point him toward the goodness and giftedness of his masculine strength. He needed to recognize and let go of the distorted images and corresponding fear of his masculine identity. As he began to imagine his masculinity in healthy ways, he would be able to embrace his strength and sexuality.

Our first prayer time was unspeakably precious. I encouraged him to confess and renounce his self-hatred and to ask Jesus to show him how Jesus saw him as a man. The Spirit led me to bless him as a man, laying hands on his back. As he looked into the eyes of Jesus, he met a gaze of immense compassion. He had never before received into his heart the blessing and compassion of any man in authority; his heart melted and he began to weep. John had many more steps to take in the healing journey, but this was the beginning of the thawing of his frozen heart so he could receive words of love and blessing on his masculine energy and strength.

John needed positive images of authority and masculinity before he could begin to embrace himself as a man. His images of men had brought only fear and self-alienation, and he needed God to heal his imagination in relation to masculinity.

Michelle was a strong Christian leader, but whenever I was around her, I could tell that she didn't like herself. People who dislike themselves or feel ashamed of their identity as a man or a woman often give off signals, sometimes even unconsciously, that undermine their influence and effectiveness in relationships. Michelle was no exception. In her immense need for affirmation of her feminine identity, she had also gotten into a sexual relationship with a man. As a result she lived with a constant sense of shame, unable to receive God's forgiveness.

At one point Michelle came to me for prayer. I felt nudged by God to pray about her body image. She was an attractive woman, but I sensed that she was very self-conscious about her body. When I asked if body image was a struggle for her, she started to weep. She had told no one, but she was constantly criticizing herself regarding her appearance. This self-criticism was rooted in her relationship with a very perfectionist mom.

As we continued to pray, Michelle confessed her rejection of herself as a woman. She wanted to be a man. She realized her parents had wanted a boy. And she had leadership gifts that her church told her she couldn't use because she was a woman. Her image of the feminine was negative and destructive, so she had cut herself off from her feminine energy and giftedness.

That day Michelle began a healing journey that has had a profound impact on her life. She invited Jesus to show her what he thought of her as a woman. In response Jesus spoke words—partly through my prayers, and partly directly to her heart—about her beauty and the delight he took in her as a woman. God began to replace her distorted images of herself with images of delight, beauty and feminine giftedness. She went on to study every healing prayer book she could get her hands on and to seek prayer at every turn.

Today Michelle is happily married and is teaching many other women to hear Jesus' affirmation of women and to imagine feminine strength and giftedness in positive, powerful ways. She likes herself as a woman, and she accepts her body as a gift from God. Such transformation is truly a miracle.

The Western church's approach to faith formation has excelled at teaching us to bring our rational thoughts under the lordship of Christ. But we have often let the devil have our imagination. The imagination and the symbols we carry in our heart are often more powerful in determining our identity and behavior than our rational thoughts, as they were for both John and Michelle.

Unless our imagination comes under the lordship of Christ, our identity will be left divided: our head may tell us one thing about who we are while our heart and imagination tell us something very different. Though we have rational knowledge of the glory of men and women, made in the image of God, many of us harbor inner pictures and symbols of men and women that are fearful, destructive, tawdry and dark, rooted in lust more than love.

Our heart-images of men and women have been shaped by advertising and other media images. Who can compete with such physical perfection? Most of the people on camera themselves don't; their images are airbrushed and adjusted electronically. What's more, traumatic experiences with men and women have often distorted our images of masculine and feminine energy and strength. Finally, our Western culture, in an attempt to establish equality and justice between the sexes, has in some ways sought to erase any sense of difference between masculinity and femininity, leaving us with little direction regarding what it means to be a healthy man or a healthy woman.

We need our imagination *sanctified,* set apart to God, made holy. So how do we recapture and renew a biblical imagination and biblical symbols for the unseen dimensions of the most important realities all around us, of God and especially of human beings?

Redemption involves restoring the defaced image of God in people. It involves the healing of our masculine and feminine dimensions and of our relationships with males and females. The biblical understand-

---

SIGNPOST 1
Learn to practice God's presence and to hear God's still small voice.

SIGNPOST 2
Replace diseased images and memories of God and human beings with healed and transformed images.

SIGNPOST 3
Renounce unreal identities. Discern and embrace your real identity.

SIGNPOST 4
Get at the roots of pain and problems, not just the fruits or symptoms.

SIGNPOST 5
Use the physical and sacramental means God has given as channels of healing power.

SIGNPOST 6
Turn outward! Healing that empowers compassion and service in the world is true healing.

---

ing of our identity and of God's power to heal has brought untold help to many sufferers, especially in areas of gender identity. If we can recover holy images, symbols and metaphors of our humanity, we will add immensely to the resources we have for healing the suffering soul.

So what does Scripture say about gender identity? Our gender identity is core to the glory of our humanity, made in the image of God, male and female. Our community as male and female in polarity and complementarity reflects the community in God's very being, existing as Father, Son and Holy Spirit.

Men are especially characterized by a relationship to work and a desire to shape their environment.[1] This focus of masculine strength and power is especially clear in the Genesis 3 account of the results of the Fall. Men experience alienation and frustration in their area of greatest authority and responsibility. They will work by the sweat of their brow and experience frustration in all that they do to bring forth fruit from the earth.

Women are especially characterized by their focus on relationships.[2] This focus of feminine strength and power becomes especially clear in the same Genesis 3 account of the Fall, where women will give birth through great pain and labor and will be ruled by men in ways that will often become a curse.

Even as the characteristic giftedness becomes the basis for the curse, the curse then leads to the characteristic sin for men and for women. Men, in order to overcome the frustration and futility they face as they work to shape their environment, often develop an inordinate and compensating drive toward power. This inordinate drive has resulted in all kinds of distorted relationships, as overbearing and authoritative men have hurt other men and women. And far too often church teaching has reinforced the characteristic sin rather than confronting it.

Women, in order to overcome the failure and pain in their relational world, have often become focused on men and children as their whole meaning for existence, bordering on idolatry. Again, far too often church teaching has reinforced such idolatry.

The corrective does not lie in rejecting all the differences between men and women but in recovering healthy, whole images and patterns of masculine and feminine strength and giftedness. I have especially been helped in this recovery by the works of C. S. Lewis, Leanne Payne and Karl Stern.[3]

When I began to see myself as a man with strength to pierce through difficulties, to speak the truth and to be the truth, to exercise courage in the face of confusion or chaos, and to embrace my particular symbolic identity as a man to serve and bless others, I began to experience transformation in my self-image. When women I have prayed for have embraced their capacity to give birth (whether or not they ever have children), their power to nurture and communicate security and acceptance, and their ability to affirm *being* over constant *doing,* I have seen their self-image begin to be transformed. As Payne reminds us, "These were once powerful images in the Western world, but are now, generally speaking, neuterized. When the great and true symbols of gender die, man and woman weaken and die too."[4]

As we recover this powerful symbolic way of seeing ourselves, how do we avoid falling into stereotypical roles and rules? For one, we need to realize that the combination of "masculine" and "feminine" symbolic qualities will differ in each of us, and ultimately each of us needs to come to a unique balance of those energies in our own soul. After all, we are more the same than we are different. Men are often called to nurture, and women are often called to lead. Second, we need to be open to the immense diversity of life as God intends it. All the gifts God gives to people need to be embraced and exercised, no matter what gender those gifts may be expressed through.

With these cautions, then, it can be profoundly healing to recover these symbolic ways of seeing ourselves. Such seeing calls us back to the core of who we are as a man or as a woman and to the purposes for which God created us in our polarity and complementarity as male and female.

BRIDGING THE HEAD AND HEART

The recovery of these symbols and metaphors will also help us encounter God and practice God's presence more deeply, though metaphors will always fall far short of the ultimate reality when it comes to speaking of God. Edwyn Bevan, in his *Symbolism and Belief,* captures well the importance of symbol and metaphor along with the humility we need to maintain as we talk about unseen things:

Act as if there were God who is a loving Father, and you will in so doing, be making the right response to that which God really is. God is really of such a character that, if any of us could know Him as He is (which we cannot do) and then had to describe in human language to those upon earth what he saw, he would have to say: "What I see is indescribable, but if you think of God as a loving Father, I cannot put the reality to you in a better way than that. That is the nearest you can get."[5]

Some people use the metaphor of God as a loving Father to "prove" that God is more masculine than feminine and that men are thus closer to the image of God than women are. That use of the metaphor is a tragedy and a travesty.

Particularly with regard to symbolic and metaphorical thinking about men and women, masculinity and femininity, we will tend to project onto God, and then back onto humanity, the cultural roles and rules we have inherited. I have become convinced that masculinity and femininity are symbols and images that call us toward health but can't give us rules and roles that limit our actions, gifts and service in the world.

Symbols and images, as Bevan's comments suggest, are the bridge between the head and the heart.[6] Symbols and images make real to us ideas and concepts about God and the human soul that otherwise would remain abstract and powerless for us. Without symbol, image and metaphor, our heart could never apprehend the truth and meaning of things, especially of unseen things, like God and the soul. When we speak of the soul or of God conceptually and abstractly, we make no heart connection. But when we speak of God as shepherd, healer, father (or nurturing mother) or lover, we enter into heart realities.

Our faith in God and our knowledge of the great Christian truths remain locked in our heads largely because we have lost or ignored metaphorical ways of knowing and thinking. We need to recover the symbolic aspects of male and female and of the image of God.

I was struck by the way the movie *The Passion of the Christ* bridged the head and the heart for many evangelical Protestants. Evangelicals emphasize that Jesus died for our sins. But that movie put flesh and blood, guts and art, into that truth. The film became a spiritual help for many believers who had not really grasped with their heart what God has done for us. Interestingly, much of the film's portrayal of Christ's passion, for instance the scourging and the journey Jesus made carrying the cross through Jerusalem, was more rooted in the Catholic imaginative and mystical tradition than in the Gospel accounts. Evangelical tradition has too often been bankrupt of symbolic power. The rejection of good and powerful symbols by some of the Protestant Reformers helps explain why some Protestant traditions have been rich in truth and head knowledge yet empty and dead in guidance for the heart toward God.

A cleansed imagination is the bridge between the head and the heart, between concept and emotional appropriation. How do we then develop the holy imagination, particularly in a world in which our imagination has been assaulted, even polluted, and in church contexts that give us very little help?

CLEANSING AND RECLAIMING THE IMAGINATION

After I make several suggestions, I will provide a prayer for the cleansing of the imagination. That prayer will help us take the first step.

The first step is to reclaim our imagination for the glory of God by placing it under the lordship of Christ. We must ask for forgiveness and cleansing for the ways we have misused and even polluted our imagination with the darkness and distortions of our world.

Nature abhors a vacuum. So the second step is to begin to fill our imagination with images of the holy, the true, the good and the beautiful. As Paul encourage us in Philippians 4:8: "Finally, brothers, whatever is true, whatever is noble, whatever is right, whatever is pure, whatever is lovely, whatever is admirable—if anything is excellent or praiseworthy—think about such things."

The filling of our heart and mind with good and beautiful and true images begins with Scripture. The stories and parables Jesus told were inherently symbolic and metaphorical. Reading the parables of Jesus fills our imagination with pictures that over time can renew and transform our thinking. The Genesis passages about the creation of men and women in the image of God and scriptural stories about healthy, God-honoring women and men will fill our heart with a vision for healthy and holy masculine and feminine qualities.

Beyond reading Scripture, we can reflect on healthy men and women we know personally. As we receive blessing and nurture from such people, these relationships can radically inform and transform our images of masculine and feminine. Our hearts are drawn to expressions of healthy masculine and feminine power and giftedness all around us. We receive into ourselves and our hearts what we admire.

A similar process happens as we read imaginative fiction. Lewis's space trilogy, J. R. R. Tolkien's Lord of the Rings trilogy, George Macdonald's Princess and Curdie series, Lewis's Narnia Chronicles and Madeleine L'Engle's Wrinkle in Time series pour out imaginative elixir, washing away the tawdry and dark and filling us with goodness and beauty. Aragorn in Lord of the Rings gives us a strong image of the masculine warrior-king, while Galadriel gives us a strong image of the feminine power to be and to be connected to the earth and the woods. Great art can have the same effect. Worship that employs the enduring Christian symbols also brings profound healing. The cross, the altar, the bread and wine of Communion, and the water of baptism all speak truths to our soul.

As we are filled with images of the good and the true, the beautiful and the holy, we can learn to listen to God and receive God's nudges and whispers through images and symbols. Often when we are broken and wounded, God's healing word in image or enacted parable will have power to heal us more deeply than words alone. You may hear God through a picture that comes to your mind's eye, or you may see a word spelled out or hear a name. You may see Jesus acting in certain ways as you pray for yourself or for others. A cleansed imagination becomes a conduit for the work and words of the Holy Spirit. Let's give our imagination to God and let God sanctify and set it apart for the healing journey.

FOR REFLECTION AND RESPONSE

Set aside a half-hour or longer for the following prayer exercise. Be in a quiet place and take uninterrupted time. If possible, surround yourself with beauty. If this is your first experience of such a prayer time, you may want someone experienced to lead you through it. A conference or small group context may be best. Now spend time in prayer, using the following as a guide.[7]

Get quiet before God. Ask for his presence to fill you and protect you. Worship Jesus and sing of his holiness. A hymn like "Holy, Holy, Holy" or a chorus like "Refiner's Fire" sets the spiritual atmosphere well. Give thanks for Jesus' death on the cross to bring forgiveness and cleansing to your imagination. Confess Jesus as Lord; tell him you belong to him and your imagination belongs to him.

Next, ask God to bring to mind images and pictures that have polluted your mind, whether lustful images from pornography, past experiences, the soft porn of TV shows and movies, violent or terrifying images, even the banality of advertising images. Let God bring to mind what God wants to cleanse and heal. Where your sinful choice gave space to the image, confess that choice for the sin that it is and ask for God's forgiveness.

Now, hold before your mind's eye Jesus with you, present to forgive and cleanse. You may see Jesus on the cross, or you may see him standing with his nail-scarred hand outstretched toward you. Place your hand on your forehead and begin to "pull out" the images that have been polluting your mind. Place those images in the hands of Jesus. You may have only a few images come to mind, or you may have many. What does Jesus do with them? What does he want to say to you about these images?

Often Jesus will show you that he has dealt with the power of these images on the cross. He has forgiven you, cleansed you and freed you from the power of such images to enslave you. So what does he do when you hand him the images? Some people see fire consume them. Others see them disappear in the cross. What comes to your mind?

Ask for the cleansing presence and power of the Holy Spirit. Ask God to claim, cleanse and fill your imagination. If you still are struggling to receive God's cleansing, go to someone you trust for prayer to help you open up to God.

Give thanks. Commit yourself in prayer to use your imaginative capacities to seek God, to be healed, to store up images of the good, the true, the beautiful and the holy.

You may want to write in a journal what you have heard and experienced, and spend time reflecting and considering next steps. You may also want to end your prayer session with worship.

Embracing Our Real Identity

Jeanne found herself torn between two poles in her sense of identity. She had always felt competent and capable, and she had always gotten a strong sense of identity in her achievements and by being told she was "the good girl." In her twenties she got married and had two kids within two years; her third child came two years later. She felt overwhelmed and inadequate, and it seemed that all she did was change diapers and burp babies. She was a very gifted, competent person who could barely keep up with these seemingly menial tasks. At times she was able to accomplish things in her home or church that revived some of her former pride in her own competency and sense of being a "good girl." At other times she was caught in feelings of self-hatred and inadequacy. Not only did she feel unproductive, but she also felt incapable of being patient, kind and loving toward her family.

At a crucial point as she swung back and forth between pride in her abilities and self-hatred of her inadequacies, she was led in a prayer session that had an immense impact. Here is her description of it:

The prayer leader suggested that some of us might need to re-move masks we had put on. I knew right away that I pro-jected this image of being all together, strong and capable and good, but it wasn't really me. It was a mask I needed to re-move. So in prayer I did. I next felt self-hatred and self-condemnation welling up in me as I focused on my weaknesses and inadequacies. I thought, *That's me. That's who I am apart from Christ.* But I sensed God telling me, "No. That's not who you are either. That's another mask. Remove that one too."

At first I argued, *Are you sure, Lord? I mean, apart from you, that's who I am.* But I continued to feel God's nudge to remove that mask too. So I did. I offered it to Jesus in my mind's eye, but then was almost afraid to look at myself and see what would be found underneath these layers.

Then I had an image of Jesus reaching out to touch me all over, and my body was radiant, filled with his light. And I heard him say, not audibly but still clearly, "When you hold your chil-dren, I hold them too. When you feed your babies, I feed them too. When you brought them forth, I was with you and in you."

At that moment I knew with my heart and not just my head that my body really is the temple of the Holy Spirit. I also knew what it meant when Jesus prayed to the Father in Gethsemane, "I am in them and you are in me" (John 14:20). And I knew with my heart what it meant for me to abide in Christ (John 15:4) and to get my identity from my abiding in Christ.

My identity is not ultimately in the first layer of self-sufficiency, nor in the second layer of self-hatred, but in this core where I remain in Jesus and he remains in me. God wanted me to *be* and not just to *do.*

I also sensed Jesus affirming my call to be a mother and his affirmation of my identity as a woman. He was addressing that part of me that I wrapped my worth in. I may not get a pay-check or a good annual review or anything that will measure my accomplishments, but Jesus dwells in me and is delighted with me as I live into my vocation of motherhood and my iden-tity as woman.

Jeanne was getting and growing a real self, as she embraced who she was in union with Christ.

Of course professional or single women won't have the same call-ing Jeanne has, but they can receive the same affirmation of their identity as they abide in Christ. So can men.

Many committed Christians talk about how our identity is in Christ and how we are a new creation; the old has passed. But in our heart and our imagination we live as if the old person, the inade-quate, failing, weak, unattractive person, is who we really are. The truth of who we are in Christ is often only a head truth for us. We do not live as if it is really true. We remain locked in old patterns, habits and addictions. And we look at ourselves from the perspective of the inner voices that judge us and reject us, not from the perspective of the divine voice that calls us toward healing and transformation.

As we learn to hear God's still small voice, we will hear other voices too. As we get quiet enough to hear God's whispers, we will get in touch with our pain and with whispers of shame, self-hatred, falling short or fear of the future that have plagued us for years. As we begin to recover the holy imagination and healthy images of God and hu-man beings, we will run into the diseased and distorted images we have harbored.

In this chapter we ask, how do we get and grow a self? How do we become a healthy person, true to who we have been created to be?

Especially we want to begin to explore how we can be healed of the lies, accusations, fears and rejections that have distorted our in-

SIGNPOST 1
Learn to practice God's presence and to hear God's still small voice.

SIGNPOST 2
Replace diseased images and memories of God and human beings with healed and transformed images.

SIGNPOST 3
Renounce unreal identities. Discern and embrace your real identity.

SIGNPOST 4
Get at the roots of pain and problems, not just the fruits or symptoms.

SIGNPOST 5
Use the physical and sacramental means God has given as channels of healing power.

SIGNPOST 6
Turn outward! Healing that empowers compassion and service in the world is true healing.

ner being. Many of these beliefs about ourselves were internalized early on. We received into our heart messages about our inadequacy, unattractiveness, failure or weakness. Many of those messages came from our primary life dialogues, dialogues with Mother and Father and other shapers of our soul and self-image.

In the back of the book you'll find an appendix on the relationship between biblical teachings on the true self and various cultural understandings of the self. If you are interested in the integration of the cultural and biblical understandings of the self, and if you are concerned about the tendency to use healing prayer primarily for the purpose of pursuing self-fulfillment, this material is crucial, especially if you are a leader. You may even want to turn to appendix one now, read it and use it as a backdrop for the material in this chapter.

WHAT'S YOUR NAME?

One of the central biblical ways to talk about identity is to focus on one's name. Names are immensely important biblically, and in many cultures they remain important today. In Scripture God's name is never to be spoken lightly or taken in vain. Jesus also tells us that if we pray for anything in his name—according to his nature and character—God the Father will hear and respond. In many cultures the naming ceremony is a central ritual, because the name implies the nature and destiny of a person.

For me one of the most moving passages in the Gospels is the account of Mary's encounter with the risen Jesus at his gravesite. She is bowed down with grief. She is anxious because she can't find the body. She is hurting because the One who gave meaning to her life is gone. She is talking with a man who she thinks is a gardener. Then Jesus speaks Mary's name. He addresses her with a tenderness and love she had often experienced from him before. He speaks to her, addressing the real her. At that moment, hearing her name, her eyes are opened, and she sees the risen Jesus with joy. In the same way, when we hear our name spoken by God's Spirit, our eyes are opened, and we recognize Jesus and receive his love.

In Scripture people often receive a new name to express their true identity. Mercurial Peter became the rock (Matthew 16:18), and God built his church on that rock. In Revelation 2:17 we are told that we will all receive a new name, a true name, written on a white stone.

What is your new name? What will you be called when you face God at the end of time or at the moment of your death? What name will capture your true identity and character and destiny?

I often ask people to imagine that Jesus is here, waiting in the next room, and wants to talk with them privately. What would he say? What would he say to you? Many people automatically suppose that Jesus' first words would convey criticism. I don't think that's true. I believe Jesus would speak our true name, as he did with Mary, and in his speaking he would love us toward our real identity, seeing the best that we are and can be. Of course, just as in Jesus' messages to the churches in Revelation 2—3, he would challenge us as well. But he would challenge us to live out of the true name that we bear, just as he challenged those seven churches to be faithful to their true name and their first love.

I know I'm speculating. But I believe I'm speculating in accord with the name, the character and nature, of Jesus.

As Lewis wrote, "How can we speak to God face to face until we have faces?"[1] His classic novel *Till We Have Faces* is a profoundly insightful exploration of the ways we can build up a false identity year by year, justifying our sin and internalizing negative words about our personhood and identity. That whole complex of the false self must be named, and we must let that false self die with Jesus on the cross. He died to free us from that false self and from those destructive inner words. As Orual, the central character of *Till We Have Faces,* comes to realize, we must all die before we die, for there is no chance after. Hell is the state in which the unreal self becomes the endless self and the false name takes over our whole identity. Imagine living forever in the false, destructive words, names and fears you have for yourself. That condition, without God, in slavery to all those destructive and deceptive words, is the condition of misery called hell. And hell has a grip on us now as long as we remain locked in negative images and destructive inner words about who we are that we received and believed from an early age. As long as we believe those voices and act accordingly, we remain immature, frustrated and stunted in our growth into personhood.

Jesus didn't die and rise again just to forgive us when we fail. He died and rose again that we might be transformed, that we might receive and believe the new name and fulfilled identity he calls us into. We become ourselves as we hear and obey God's healing and directing word. As we act in accord with our true name and our real identity, we become who we were created to be. As Paul puts it in Ephesians 4:22-24:

> You were taught, with regard to your former way of life, to put off [one-time act] your old self, which is being corrupted by its deceitful desires; to be made new [ongoing act] in the attitude of your minds; and to put on [one-time act] the new self, created to be like God in true righteousness and holiness.

We got a new self, which is our real self, through our union with Christ. God made his home in us. We are his new temple, individually and corporately. When the Spirit took up residence in us, God made union with us, as Jeanne so deeply realized in the story that began this chapter.

As Leanne Payne has put it, "Another lives in us."[2] That is the secret of the Christian life. As Christians each of us is a new being, a new creation,[3] produced by the union of God's Spirit with our spirit. This new creation is the determining fact of our existence, the basic ground of our identity. We get it as a gift.

Now we need to become as adults what we already are in infancy. The life energy is there. The new identity is there. We merely need to choose to see it, embrace it, live in the reality of what we already are and have been given. Of course, it takes all of our effort to live in that reality, because the unreal identities within us get considerable attention and nurture from the world around us and from the puppet-master of this world system, the devil.

How do we identify the unreal self, the destructive words about who we are and the deceptive things we have believed about ourselves? How do we then hear and embrace our true name, our real identity? Where do we get the strength and wisdom to live in accord with that true identity, free of the addictive ways we have fed our unreal self and numbed our pain? These questions will be addressed in the next several chapters. We will first explore how to identify unreal selves and how to begin to break free of their dominance. We will receive strengthening for our willpower, which may have become weak through feeding an unreal self and avoiding pain.

Then we will look at the source of many of the false and destructive words we have received into our hearts by considering the power of our dialogue with Mother and Father to shape our souls. In those chapters we will learn how to get at the roots of our struggles rather than just the symptoms. Pornography, unhealthy dependent relationships, sexual addiction, food addictions, alcoholism and obsessive fantasy life are all the fruits, the symptoms of inner distortions of our identity. Rooted in destructive beliefs and words about ourselves, these are unhealthy ways of meeting valid needs. They distort our inner life, sometimes until it becomes a living hell of misery and endless self-talk.

Through the whole process of renouncing unreal identities, the image and vision of our God-created real identity, given birth through our union with Christ, can light the way with hope.

THE REAL AND UNREAL SELF

In this book I use the terms *real* and *unreal* to refer to the biblical understanding and approach to the self. Other people have used other terms. Some speak of the "true self" versus the "false self." The true self is the new self in Christ. The false self is the old man or old woman within us, the self that is subject to sin, Satan and death. One problem with "true self/false self" language is our tendency to use it statically, as if there were only one true self. The "true self" is always becoming, being transformed toward the image of Christ. Thus there is not just one "true" self but innumerable possibilities, based on many factors including our background, our choices, God's presence and purposes in our life, our relationships with others, our culture and community, and our personal gifts, capacities and opportunities. "Real self" language points to our growing and becoming in ways consistent with our God-given identity and capacities, but it leaves open the possibility of many different directions in which we can grow and become.

Another way to describe the self then is to talk about "authentic" versus "adaptive or addictive" selves. *Authentic* self can be a good synonym for the real self. An authentic self is true to who God has made us to be and also true to our community, background and opportunities. An *adaptive* self has primarily been engendered out of adapting to pain, brokenness, the expectations and needs of others—out of our addictive and comforting ways of coping with stress and pain. The adaptive self is the self we project for others. Of course, on one level we are always adapting. Our community and the expectations of those around us can help shape our identity in healthy and good ways, not just in negative ways. But we can put on an outer self and image that distorts our integrity and identity, alienating us from who we are created to be. This adaptive or addictive self is an unreal creation, an expression of our neediness instead of our health.

The language of authentic versus adaptive may be most helpful for you; if so, feel free to think in those terms. You will find more help on understanding real and unreal selves in appendix one, "On Biblical and Cultural Sources of the Self."

FOR REFLECTION AND RESPONSE
Once again, set aside uninterrupted time in a safe place conducive to prayer and hearing from God.

Consider with God: What might your new name be? Spend time listening to God, asking God how he names you and what most delights him about you. If you have trouble hearing anything, consider what might block you from hearing God's affirmation of you.

Also, consider what *you* might want your real name to be. God often has planted the seeds of what we will become in our deepest desires. So take seriously what you desire your name to be. Ask God what might help you grow into that name.

Renouncing Unreal Identities

Christine was a bright and gifted member of a campus fellowship group. She joined a small group and started growing in her faith. Her roommate was also her small group leader, and as time passed they became very close. They shared their thoughts and feelings. They took similar classes. They shared clothes and possessions. As they became closer, Christine found increasing amounts of energy were being invested in thinking about her roommate; she started seeing her emotional life go up and down as her relationship with this friend went up and down.

Sharing thoughts and feelings led to hugs and other physical expressions of affection. Christine began losing her sense of where she ended and her friend began. Emotional boundaries and perspective were dissipating. Finally, physical boundaries disappeared. Sharing feelings, clothes and possessions led to sharing beds. They became involved with each other sexually, not because they were initially oriented that way but because it was natural for their emotional enmeshment to become physical enmeshment.

After several years in the lesbian lifestyle, Christine began the painful process of making different choices and seeking healing. Though she had not initially been oriented sexually toward women, her emotional enmeshment and sexual expression made it very difficult and very painful to change.

Christine's struggle was not first of all sexual; it was emotional. Her struggle was *idolatry,* enmeshment with another woman in order to provide an inner sense of who she was. Christine had to begin by rejecting this unreal identity and addictive relationship. Until she renounced her idolatry and enmeshment, she had very little capacity to hear from God about her real identity.

I am not saying that all homosexual relationships are like Christine's. But Christine needed to begin with renunciation as she abandoned an unreal and addictive identity in order to ultimately embrace her real identity. She did so with the support of loving friends and a praying community, and today she has experienced healing and transformation on many levels.

The journey of embracing our real identity often begins when we renounce unreal identities. When there is an addictive and controlling pattern that we keep falling back into, there is no room for the real to enter and become solid. Continually returning to pornography, food, addictive sex, fantasy, emotional enmeshment or any other source of momentary comfort, our inner life is trapped in a vicious cycle. We are ashamed of our neediness, and we fight against the addictive pattern or unhealthy form of comfort. But in a moment of pain or vulnerability we fall again, and we continue to live in shame for who we are, what we have done and how needy we are. That cycle keeps us from progressing in a healthy self-view and achieving a healthy inner life.

Whenever we fall into an unhealthy pattern of numbing pain and finding comfort, we are looking to another person or thing to tell us who we are and that we are okay. We may be looking to another person, an authority figure or a peer. We may be seeking comfort in an object or a repeated experience that makes us forget for a while the anxiety that wracks us. Christine followed this pattern in her relationship with her roommate.

BENTNESS: AN IMAGE FOR IDOLATRY

We are helped here again by C. S. Lewis, and by Leanne Payne who built on his work. Lewis called any inordinate focus on other things and people the "bent over position."[1] We bend toward another person or thing, asking that person or thing to tell us we are okay and to nurture our sense of well-being. That person or thing plays a large role in our inner life, both when we are getting the sense of comfort and when we are recovering afterward.

Dependent relationships are an obvious example. We become dependent on another person, bent over, seeking from them something we lack within. When we are with that person, we feel okay about ourselves. When we are apart, we feel empty, inadequate, incomplete. When we are with them, we are constantly aware of what they are doing and what messages they are sending to us. We notice their interactions with others, and we often feel jealous when they are having too good a time and enjoying themselves too much with someone else.

There are many other examples. Any sexual struggle can be looked at similarly as involving a bent-over position toward that thing, person or experience. We are too focused on it or them. Always we are fighting not to do it again, or doing it again, or recovering and feeling shame about doing it again. The person, thing or experience has far too strong a hold on our thought-and-feeling life. We can be addicted to money or power in the same way.

When I took a sabbatical from my job, I had to face my own inner emptiness in a new light. I was used to defining my identity and feeling good about myself on the basis of my job—doing things for which other people valued and affirmed me. Meaningful work is a very good thing, but I wasn't able to feel good about myself when I stopped working for a time and lost the affirmation that I had constantly fed on. I discovered that I was bent over toward work and affirmation.

We can be bent over toward money, feeling secure only in times of financial advance. When we lack that security we feel anxious about money and hold onto it, always hedging our bets. Money is a good servant but a bad master.

We can be in the bent-over position with a husband or wife. We were meant to be one and to depend on each other in a healthy way. But when we look to that relationship to define our identity and we feel good about ourselves only when that person gives us attention, we are riding too much on that person and relationship. We are bent over.

Some church traditions have taught women that their identity is found only in their husband and in their role as wives. This teaching is a reinforcement of the bent-over position. Here my point is not to argue for an egalitarian view of marriage but to argue against any view of marriage that keeps one partner dependent on the other and not maturing in Christ. We are all to be in the *upright* position, looking to Jesus for our ultimate identity and the truest word about who we are. And we are all responsible before God to make decisions, maintain integrity of conscience and obey God rather than human beings.

We can be bent over toward our body image. Maybe we wrap our identity up in having a good physique, or maybe we are obsessed with the ways our body doesn't measure up. Either way, body image has become an idol toward which we are bent.

The Bible's word for the bent-over position is *idolatry.* We are looking to another person or thing to tell us who we are.

We are called to repent of sin, renounce idols, and ask God to redeem and set in order genuine human needs that have become distorted and misdirected. I believe we have so focused on repenting of sin as the only key to transformation that we have missed other vital dimensions. We are right to turn away from sin, which is our choice to go our own way rather than God's. But equally important, we must *renounce and reject* idolatries and unreal identities. Renunciation is the act of verbally and willfully turning away from what we have idolized and giving ourselves to God instead. This practice is critical for the health of the Christian life and the fashioning of a true identity.

Renunciation does *not* involve rejecting the genuine and God-given needs that lie behind many of our idolatries. We ask God to redeem them, to set in order those needs, so that worship of God is always preeminent and so that our needs are expressed and met in ways that fit our God-given identity rather than distorting it.

When we have spent time in the bent-over position, we will find that our will to fight the addiction or unhealthy pattern has weakened. We need to get free enough of what we have been enslaved to so that we can begin to get healthy and feed our needs with good and healthy choices. But how do we feed and strengthen our willpower to fight? How do we weak-willed people begin to find the will to be free and healthy?

IDOLATRY IN MEN AND WOMEN

I want to suggest a teaching and prayer process that has helped many people. First, we must teach the biblical truths of our God-created, God-redeemed identity as men and women in Christ. People need to know that they are a new creation, that the old self has died with Christ, that they have been raised to new life and that the Spirit empowers them to live in accordance with who they already are.

Second, we must help people understand the characteristic idolatries and forms of bentness that they may experience as a man or a woman. Genesis 1—3 contains some profound teaching on gender-specific forms of bentness.

In Genesis 3 men are told they will work by the sweat of their brow. Men are frustrated in their life of work, never finding the fulfillment and fruitfulness that they were made to experience. Thus men tend to be bent toward their work. They are also bent toward the approval of other men, especially their father. Ultimately this frustrated need has its root in the fall from favor with their heavenly Father. Unaffirmed men are unable to affirm other men. Unaffirmed fathers are unable to affirm their sons. And so the cycle goes on, down through generations. Men tend to wrap up their identity in their work and in the approval of other men. In an extreme form, the need for the approval of other men, and ultimately of the father, can lead to workaholism in one man and addictive homosexual practice in another.

Men in our culture have also suffered a loss of mothering. As a result, men can also be bent toward women, toward sex and pornography. Casual sex and pornography can be false, ultimately unsatisfying and addictive ways of connecting to the feminine need for nurture, well-being and even being itself.

Male idolatry is often visual. Men tend to be more visual; they often have a great need for the cleansing of their imagination, given their temptations toward masturbation and an intense fantasy life. Men keep the pornography business thriving.[2]

Women are told in Genesis 3 that their desire will be for their husband. This is not the God-given desire expressed after their initial creation but the frustrated desire that characterizes our relationships today. Women are tempted to find their identity in a relationship with a man. They can feel they are not a whole person if they are not in such a relationship. Their bentness is often toward men and the approval and attention of men.

Female idolatry is often emotional and relational. Their temptation is to build relationships of emotional dependency and enmeshment. They also face the temptation to give themselves away physically in order to get what they need emotionally. Women keep the romantic fantasy business thriving.[3]

With the diminishment of mothering in our day and the tendency of unaffirmed men to hurt or abuse their daughters, women can also turn away from men entirely, seeking affirmation from and practicing emotional dependency with other women.

You may want to take a moment now to reflect on your own forms of bentness. To whom or what do you look to tell you that you are okay and to give you a sense of worth and well-being?

Third, we must teach people a prayer process that helps them regularly appropriate God's power to live in their real identity and to renounce unreal identities and the bent-over posture. That process includes several steps:

- reaffirming and reconnecting to our union with Christ

- renouncing and forsaking our idolatries and unreal identities

- aligning our will with God's will and allowing our will to be strengthened

- looking to God for healing and filling

- choosing to meet our valid needs in God-given ways

As we invite God to minister to hurting souls, our own and others', using this prayer process, God will transform us. The prayers below flesh out this process; they can be prayed alone, with a prayer partner or with a group. Only after God has led your own soul through the process can you lead others. It would be a mistake to start leading others too quickly. To have the wisdom to lead others well, we must learn the skill of listening to God and must have experienced some real transformation in these areas of our own lives.

The process requires the work of God's Spirit and is carried on primarily in community. We Protestants have disregarded the impor-

tance of confessing our sins to one another, of receiving the pro-
nouncement of forgiveness from one another. James 5:16 is clear: our
experience of forgiveness, healing and transformation is tied to our
confession of sins and prayers for healing with one another. We can
be channels of God's healing and transformation to one another
through confession, prayer, laying on of hands and the appropriate
meeting of genuine needs.

Learning to walk daily in our real identity in Christ is a long obedience in the same direction. Often we face a besetting idolatry, a besetting sin. This area of greatest struggle is often related to some deep
rejection or hurt. At places of profound hurt, the temptation toward
idolatry is great. We need continually to recognize our bentness, renounce it, worship God and practice his presence, and commit ourselves to relationships of love, encouragement and accountability
with others who know us and our darker side. As we do, we will experience the progressive transformation that we long for and that will
be winsome and contagious to others. We will have an ever new, ever
fresh story of transformation to tell.

FOR REFLECTION AND RESPONSE

Here is a guide for practicing God's presence, turning away from false
identities and receiving a real identity in God.

First, practice God's presence and tune your ears and your heart to
his voice. Pray and affirm the truths that Jesus spoke:

> Before long, the world will not see me anymore, but you will see
> me. Because I live, you also will live. On that day you will real-
> ize that I am in my Father, and you are in me, and I am in you.
> . . . If anyone loves me, he will obey my teaching. My Father will
> love him, and we will come to him and make our home with
> him. (John 14:19-20, 23)

Another lives in you. Alleluia! The God of the universe, the Creator of planets and stars, the Redeemer who died for you and now lives and reigns, is one with you by the Spirit! How can you not experience healing and transformation? Take time to rejoice in this.

Now repent of your unreal identities. Renounce false images of yourself, which are forms of idolatry. They will have spiritual power over you until you do. But do not repent of your created human needs; repent of any inhuman and self-centered ways you have sought to meet those needs. Seek the strengthening of your will, which has been weakened by the practice of idolatry and dependency. You may need emotional divorces from past and present dependent and sexually involved relationships. (These next prayers, especially for the strengthening of the will, are adapted from Payne's *Healing Presence*, p. 64.)

I pray, Lord, for the release and strengthening of my will, with which I initiate change and choose life, and with which I forsake the bent, idolatrous position of attempting to find my identity in other people or other things.

Show me any way in which I am bent toward the creature. O Lord, reveal any idolatrous dependency on persons or things; show me any way I demand from the created the identity I can gain only from you, my Creator.

Visualize (see with your heart) any bentness the Lord is showing you. Then see yourself deliberately straightening up from that idol as you pray:

I choose, Lord, to forsake this bentness. I confess it to you as the sin, the idol, that it is. I renounce it in your name. I renounce it in your name. And I thank you for your forgiveness. I receive your forgiveness and cleansing.

Rejoice in the promise: *To those who truly repent, I proclaim you forgiven, in Christ's name. Receive this forgiveness now into your heart.* Then pray:

Come into me, divine, initiating, eternal Will. Lord, command what you will, and then will what you command.

I thank you, Lord, that my weak and insufficient will is now one with yours. May I know more and more what it means to be in-willed, indwelt by you. Thank you, Lord, that your completing, healing work is begun in me and will continue in this world and the next.

Write in your prayer journal the images of bentness you saw toward mother or father, husband or wife, son or daughter, someone of the same sex or other sex, any way you have made an idol of job, money, fame or self. Then converse with God about them. He will give you understanding of them and enable you to get at the roots of the idolatries or dependencies that have held you back from full freedom in him.

Now visualize the cross between you and the person or thing you were bent toward. See Jesus coming between you and that person, setting a holy boundary, protecting you from hurtful or dependency-building acts and words. Now see yourself giving the pieces of their heart back to this person—pieces of their heart that weren't theirs to give you. See yourself taking back the pieces of *your* heart that weren't yours to give this person. You can tell that person what you are doing and why, and you can ask their forgiveness, and extend yours, for the emotional or physical union that was not healthy or appropriate.

Celebrate, give thanks to God for his mighty presence with you and within you. Pray:

God, fill me now with your light and your love. Replace the distorted images and dependent relationships. Fill me with your presence, with your light, with images of the good and the true and the beautiful. Spirit of God, now fill me from the bottom of my toes to the top of my head; fill every cell of my being with your presence, as if filling a glass with clear water. Come, Holy Spirit. Fill me and use me, I pray. I give you all thanks and all glory and all praise.

I choose now to meet my God-given needs in God-glorifying and health-giving ways. And I ask, Lord, that you will teach me to minister to others in the way you are now ministering to me. For I pray in your name. Amen.

The Dialogue with Mother and Father

In many ways the next five chapters lie at the heart of this book and the journey we are on together. In these chapters you will receive many prayers and much help for your deepest struggles and hurts. Let me begin by sharing with you some positive stories of relating to my mom and dad as illustrations of the power of positive dialogue with mother and father. I give thanks to God for their role in my life.

One of my earliest memories goes back to an early morning in Vermont. When I was four, my dad awoke me at 5:00 a.m. and took me down the stairs of our two-flat and back to the shed. He directed me to gather some night crawlers, and we drove off to a small lake nearby. He hoisted a canoe on his shoulders and encouraged me to help carry it by holding onto the back, where the canoe came to a point. I felt I was really contributing; in retrospect, I imagine his main concern was that I not wander off, so he wanted me to hang on and think I was helping.

We launched the canoe into the lake, and I proceeded to catch more fish that day than Dad did. No doubt the fact that he spent half his day taking off my fish and helping me bait my hook affected the final tally. But who cared? I caught more fish than Dad!

He affirmed me deeply that day, telling me that he had not caught more fish than his own dad until he was late in his teens. Was I a man or what? My little four-year-old chest swelled with pride and a sense of accomplishment. My dad blessed me that day.

One of my earliest memories of my mother also dates back to the year I was four. One day I was sick in bed, and I remember how my mother came to me, took my temperature, worried over me, made me comfortable, brought me saltine crackers and ginger ale. She nurtured me. She didn't expect me to grit my teeth and act as if nothing was wrong. She wanted me to rest. She gave me permission to be weak. She loved me in my weakness and need and expressed her love even more than usual.

A nurturing mother pours love generously into our soul. We are loved even when we're not pretty!

My parents have often said that their biggest source of conflict had to do with how to bring us up. My dad is a Marine. We moved around a lot when I was young, partly because of his involvement in the Marine Corps. He used to lightly punch us boys in the shoulder and ask, "Does that hurt?" The correct response was, "No!" whether it hurt or not. When he asked, "Why not?" we were to shout out, "Because I'm a Marine!" That little ritual began very early on, and so I was a very young Marine! My dad was from the "Spare the rod and spoil the child" school of childrearing.

In contrast, my brothers and I used to laugh ourselves silly when my mom threatened to spank us. She has never been able to hurt someone smaller than she is. She often let Dad know when she thought he crossed a line in physical harshness with us.

I am glad we had the balance. In addition, my mother stood up for us, and her mother-love included a fierce desire to protect us. This was a powerful shaper of my soul.

Many of our personal strengths and many roots of our struggles and sins lie deep in the soil of the primary relationships of our lives, relationships with our mother and father or with those who played their roles. Of course, many others played significant roles as well. Here, however, we will focus our attention on these two primary relationships.

When our interactions with our mother and father were healthy and life-giving, our soul was shaped in strong and healthy ways. When interactions with our mother and father were distorted, this dialogue gave a distorted shape to our soul.

As Martin Buber has said with simple eloquence, we become persons as we engage in I-Thou dialogue, as opposed to I-It dialogue, first with others and ultimately with *the* Other, God.[1] We become as we listen to God and obey his voice. We become as we respond to his word to us about who we are. God can expose the lies and false words about who we are and speak the true words about who we are, our true name, into our soul.

A baby knows that he is, and knows that it is good that he is, when he sees joy in his mother's eyes. The baby doesn't even know where he ends and his mother begins. The I-Thou dialogue with Mother is the first great dialogue of his life. When the dialogue is healthy, the young soul knows he is loved. Nothing is more basic. When the dialogue is disordered, the small person is filled with primal anxiety, an anxiety that will distort every relationship he ever has.

A teen girl knows that she is attractive to boys and men first in the eyes of her father. His hug, his words, his affirmation teach her that she is loved and worthy of love. But when Father is abusive or distant, she will become defensive or driven—the effects will be evident in every relationship she has with men.

These primal dialogues form the root of personhood and soul in-

---

SIGNPOST 1
Learn to practice God's presence and to hear God's still small voice.

SIGNPOST 2
Replace diseased images and memories of God and human beings with healed and transformed images.

SIGNPOST 3
Renounce unreal identities. Discern and embrace your real identity.

SIGNPOST 4
Get at the roots of pain and problems, not just the fruits or symptoms.

SIGNPOST 5
Use the physical and sacramental means God has given as channels of healing power.

SIGNPOST 6
Turn outward! Healing that empowers compassion and service in the world is true healing.

---

tegrity. I have described some positive images of the affirming father and the nurturing mother. But we also need to explore other images that often lie behind the struggles we experience.

THE ABSENT FATHER AND DISTANT MOTHER

My dad has been a very successful educator. He grew up in a generation in which mothers stayed home and fathers went out into the world to make their way and provide for their family. My dad founded a community college and has gone on to teach at Arizona State University and now New York University. His busy and responsible professional life kept him traveling often when I was in my teen years.

His example had a profound impact on me for good. I cannot

imagine living without contributing to the world around me. And I work hard partly because my dad worked hard and still does. But at a deep level I often felt as if Dad was neither present for me nor proud of me. My soul longed for his affirmation.

A later memory of my mother comes from when I was in my teens. At that point Mom had been a mother for many years. A very gifted and competent woman, she had begun to coordinate the League of Women Voters and, it seemed to me, a lot of the rest of the world.

That example was helpful and inspiring to me in many ways. I have immense respect for the gifts and capacities of women and deeply believe that women, just like men, ought to be able to serve, lead and contribute in whatever ways their gifts make possible. But sometimes, even in the healthiest of homes and with the best of moms, we still need healing.

I have struggled with an ever-present static, a background of anxiety, because I was disconnected from the nurture and security of Mom earlier than I would have liked. A big step in the process of disconnection happened early on, when my two brothers were born while I was three. After Mom got them squared away (that certainly took a few years!), she began to turn her attention to professional and volunteer pursuits. These were very good choices. It wasn't that she did anything inappropriate for a mother. She was a very good mom. But despite growing up in a relatively good home, with very good parents, I have needed to come to terms with long-term anxieties and inadequacies that have become part of the shape of my own soul.

We all inhabit a fallen world. We will all need to face the distortions in the shape of our own soul and to seek healing.

Another example comes from my own parenting. I have a tendency to become very focused in my inner world of thoughts, images and insights. Of course, that tendency helps me write. But sometimes my kids experience me as being distant, unavailable and reserved because my mind is elsewhere even when my body is present. Even as I am writing this paragraph, my youngest son is letting me know he wants my attention, and he is making it very clear that sometimes when he needs to talk to me he finds me lost in another world!

My kids would all say I am a good dad. There is a lot of love in our family. And of course I battle to be as present as possible for those closest to me. I am responsible and continue to seek to grow in my areas of sin and weakness. But I am still fallen as a father. No doubt my kids will someday receive prayer for God's blessing and healing presence because their dad was off somewhere in his own little world at a time when they needed his attention and blessing.

THE ABUSIVE FATHER AND CONTROLLING MOTHER

Many people have had challenging experiences with an abusive father or a controlling mother. My friend Shelley was abused not physically but emotionally. She never knew what her dad would say or do next. She was often surprised by his selfishness and his criticism when she didn't meet his needs or fulfill his expectations.

I have also prayed for many women who experienced sexual abuse in their childhood or youth and have had to deal with the violence of that violation. Many experienced the only attention they ever really got during such moments, so they both hated and longed for repetition of the abuse.

Many men who are unable to commit themselves to a relationship with a woman, or who find intimacy with a woman difficult, had a controlling mother when they were growing up. For some reason Mom had strong needs attached to the relationship with her son and manipulated him to get it or keep it. Maybe Dad was absent or had abandoned the marriage or was very distant emotionally. Whatever the reason, Mom needed something from her child that the child wasn't yet able to give. So the child felt enmeshed with Mom and eventually needed to escape. Often I have seen men unable to commit to a wife because the strings attached to Mom are still too thick and sticky.

MOTHERS GIVE BEING AND WELL-BEING

When the interactions with our mother are healthy, we gain a sense of being and well-being at our core.[2] Picture a child at her mother's breast. The child suckles, taking nourishment into her little body. She burps (cutely) and then snuggles satisfied against Mom. She is content. There is nothing to worry about, no need that she has that is insatiable. She is cared for, nurtured, protected and safe. She has a sense of being: she senses that she exists and that her existence is a supremely good thing. She has a sense of well-being as well: all is right with the world.

Birthday celebrations announce clearly that it is a good thing that we exist. Did you ever think about that? Birthday celebrations are not tied to anything we have done or accomplished; birthdays celebrate that we *are*. If as you were growing up your birthday was forgotten or minimized, you may well have very little sense of celebration that you are and that your existence is to be rejoiced over.

When the connection with Mom is severed immediately after birth or very early, and no mother substitute comes forward, people grow up with a primal question about whether they even exist. I have prayed with sufferers who wonder whether there is anything real about themselves or their world at all.

FATHERS GIVE BLESSING

Fathers bless our sense of competence and gender identity.[3] Mom creates the circle of belonging, and Dad calls the growing boy or girl out of that circle into the bigger world.

Often the voice inside us that tells us if we're competent, or if we're a solid man or an attractive woman, is Dad's voice. Mother has given us being, even from the womb. Father, or people who stand in the place of Dad, give us blessing.[4] It is a father's proud smile we often look for after a significant accomplishment, and we often need a father's hug or affirmation of our gender identity.

Mom may be most crucial in the first ten years, when we pour the foundations for a healthy identity. Dad is often more crucial in the next ten years, when we build up the ground floor of our vocational and relational life.

Additionally, how Mom and Dad interacted, if we had both parents, profoundly affects us. Often children's perceptions are deeply influenced by the ways Mom or Dad interprets the other parent to them. Great discernment is needed as we pray with people about their growing-up experiences, especially as they sort out the interplay between perception and reality. I have prayed with many sufferers who can only see their Mom or their Dad through the eyes of the other parent, causing additional layers of distortion.

What happens when interactions with mother or father or both were disordered or destructive? How do we understand the fruits of our problems by looking at these roots? And how do we find healing for the soul that has become distorted by a disordered primal dialogue? These questions will be explored in the next two chapters.

FOR REFLECTION AND RESPONSE

1. Think back on experiences that provided you with good images of a mom or a dad, of nurture or affirmation. Even the most difficult home situation probably held a few good things. Give thanks for these.

2. Which negative images of parents did you most connect with? What impact do you think they had on you?

Healing Mother Wounds

Tom could not remember a time when he hadn't felt anxious about the future and about relationships. He was part of a prayer team I led for a missions conference and was excited about praying for others. But he also knew he needed God's touch at a deep place in his being. He told me that he often felt empty, as if he was hardly there, and as if it didn't really matter anyway. He also struggled with an almost obsessive focus on women's breasts. For years he had tried to repress that obsessive focus, but it hadn't lessened. He had come to realize that the obsessive focus on breasts wasn't primarily sexual. It was a deep longing to receive nurture and to be filled with a sense of being and well-being.

When he was still in his mother's womb, his father got very sick with colon cancer. Throughout the pregnancy Tom's mother was deeply frightened. Two months after Tom was born, his father died. His mother, caught in grief, was incapable of giving Tom attention or nurture during his infancy and toddler years. Tom suffered seriously from a lack of a sense of being and well-being.

At one point during our conference, Tom realized that he needed prayer, and he began to prepare himself. Here is his account of receiving prayer for being and well-being:

> Sitting around our tables at breakfast with our healing prayer team, I began to feel invisible. Like a wallflower. I knew now that this was what it means not to have a sense of being.
>
> It was our last morning, and I was beginning to grow anxious that I would miss my moment with God. As I thought about this, a picture came into my heart. I saw a bloody mess, and then, a newborn baby wrapped in a white blanket. But the baby was black, not because of skin pigmentation but because it was dead. I sought out MaryKay, and she invited Anne to join us for healing prayer.
>
> I told them the short version of my story and described the images of my difficult birth and sense of being unwanted. These two caring women just listened for a while, not saying or praying a word. God led them to pray for what I had experienced even in the womb. I had a sense that it was in the womb that the baby (me) had lost a sense of being.
>
> They invited me to listen to the Spirit, to ask God what God wanted to say to that baby in the womb. At first I saw a woman (my mother), lying down, pregnant, with her full round womb exposed. She was safe and protected. It is so hard to describe my feelings at that moment. So much comes at you in a moment of seeing truth symbolically, and to unpack that moment is to unpack so many feelings and so much meaning. But what I remember most is that this beautiful woman loved her baby in her womb, and I knew it was true. The later pain and grief overwhelmed the love for a time, but I knew that she had started with love.
>
> Then from inside the womb, I saw two large hands come

from the sky. God's hands touched my mother gently and then entered her womb and took hold of me with great love. This picture made so real to my heart the truth of Psalm 139:13 that even from the womb God knew me, loved me, wanted me.

He kept his hands upon me for a long while, and I just sank under the peace of it. Every fiber in my body began to relax as he filled me, and then, in the small of my back, I felt heat, penetrating but also comforting. I could have stayed there for hours, days. I had become like my own son feeding upon his mother's breast, lying limp and satiated in his mother's arms.

After a time, I shared with MaryKay and Anne what I was experiencing. They continued listening to God. Then they began to pray for me in a new way. They saw me as like a tree, a large oak whose branches went deep into the earth. When I moved, the whole root system moved with me. I had been reading Psalm 1 about the man who obeys being like a tree whose roots go deep. God was answering my prayers and my heart longing.

As I rose from the prayer time, I sensed the roots, and I had, maybe for the first time in my life, a deep sense of being and well-being. I knew that I was, and I knew that it was deeply good that I was, that I existed. I returned to my room, lay down upon my bed, basked in the presence of God, and, over the next few days, broke out into spontaneous laughter often, just for the joy of being alive.

God brought deep healing for Tom that morning. To receive it, he had needed to understand what he was struggling with. Too often people struggling with sexuality, gender identity, food addictions, alcohol or other comfort experiences focus on the symptoms and not the roots of their struggles.

What *are* the roots? If mothers give being and well-being, what are the consequences if the interaction with Mom was disordered, distant or destructive? When being or well-being is absent or insufficient, we experience some or all of the following consequences.

Separation Anxiety

Anxiety is a feeling of unease, often without any clear focus.[1] We feel worried. We feel uncomfortable. We are always waiting for the other shoe to drop.

For some people, anxiety forms a constant life background, as it did for Tom. They are always a bit on edge. Whenever they get quiet, they are not at peace but worried, often without even knowing what they are concerned about.

Often the root of such constant anxiety and lack of peace is early separation from one's mother. Mom wasn't there to give a sense of security, peace and well-being. Needs for her presence, comfort and nurture went unmet, leading to a life of anxiety.

In some cases our mother had no choice. It used to be common in hospitals to separate mother and child for a significant time after birth. Some children are born with a serious illness. One of my dear friends was born premature and spent a month hooked up to wires in the hospital. Imagine a little one, safe and nurtured and protected in the womb, who enters the world and is then cut off from contact, nurture and comfort from a mother for long periods of time. Such an experience can lead to primal loneliness and ceaseless anxiety. But the baby has no way to understand the experience or cope with it. Into adulthood that person can feel vaguely or even intensely uneasy about all of life without really knowing why.

Some mothers simply do not have a capacity to love and nurture. Another close friend of mine recently had an image of her mother as a skeleton, no flesh, no nurture to give.

Some mothers abandon their children.

The root of anxiety can go very deep in the person separated too early from Mother. It is like a constant static in every relationship and experience. When a child has experienced intense anxiety over losing Mom's nurture and presence, the child often carries a deep fear of rejection. People with separation anxiety desperately need love but are profoundly afraid of rejection. Sometimes they may cling; at other times they reject others before they can be rejected. Either way, they often fulfill their own fears of being alone.

COMFORT SEEKING

When we feel anxious, we long to be comforted. We want the uneasiness to go away. At a deep level, we are wracked with pain from the loss of Mother's nurture and the sense of rejection. We want to forget the pain or escape it for a while. So we seek comfort, sometimes in healthy ways, sometimes in destructive ways.

The roots of many addictions lie in the soil of loss and pain based in separation anxiety. Addictive experiences give us substitutes for the real thing. We longed for acceptance, love and nurture. We didn't receive it, and we don't believe we can. We may feel unworthy of being loved. We may be so sure we will be rejected that we are unable to take the risk. So we protect ourselves and our heart from the potential for rejection that comes with committed, loving relationships. Instead we turn to experiences that give us pleasure or a surge of excitement to mask our pain and provide a substitute sense of well-being.

Comfort for men is often visual and sexual. Men try to fill the inner emptiness with adrenaline. Men can turn to pornography for a "risk-free" sense of comfort. When you pay for sex or pornography, you will be stroked and you don't have to worry about rejection. Of course it is all illusion. There is no real love or nurture, only a temporary sense of release and an adrenaline rush.

One man I worked with for several years was so disconnected from Mom that he sought a sense of being, a sense that he was actually there, by plunging into ever more intense sexual experiences. An intense feeling could convince him, at least momentarily, that he was really there. He started with pornography in magazines, then moved to the Internet, then gentlemen's clubs and finally prostitutes. At the moment of the sexual charge he felt alive. But the sense of being alive was illusory. His real need was for his mom's love, commitment and nurture. The tragedy is that as we feed our cravings on the charge, real life seems less and less potent and satisfying. This man's need became more and more intense and insatiable as he tried to meet it in these illusory ways.

Steps toward healing always involve finding a support system and then getting off the addiction. Until we stop depending on the charge, our life will have no room for the real.

Comfort for women is often emotional. Women often try to fill an inner emptiness by filling up with good feelings. They can become emotionally enmeshed and dependent on others, men or women. Or they may seek a release of good feelings through eating or immersing themselves in some other comfort activity.

As I've prayed with women who struggle with lesbianism, I have learned that many of them were not initially seeking the sexual dimension, only the emotional. As Christine puts it (see chapter nine), she started by sharing her thoughts and feelings with her college roommate; they went on to share clothes, vacations and finally each other's bed. The sexual relationship was merely the last step in the process of emotional enmeshment and dependency. Sometimes at the root of this process is this profound need for comfort and nurture and love that we long to receive from our mother. And whether a relationship ever becomes sexual or not, emotional dependency and enmeshment must be faced and overcome.

Comfort is a good thing. But what we choose to turn to for comfort is crucial.

One final dimension of comfort seeking: often we will try to connect with something in another person that is present but unaffirmed in ourselves. Men who seek sex with other men may be trying to connect with the unaffirmed masculine part of themselves, but their effort will ultimately be self-defeating. People who seek sex and connection with a dependent, needy person may be trying to connect with a needy, dependent part of themselves that was unaffirmed and rejected. Pedophiles are often trying to connect with a missing or unaffirmed childhood. Such misguided attempts are indications of the real thing that we long for. Healing has to do with turning from misguided and destructive attempts and beginning to seek real affirmation of and real connection with those parts of ourselves.

Commitment Avoidance

If Mom was smothering, we can have great difficulty committing ourselves to romantic relationships in adulthood. I have often counseled men in their thirties who have had a series of romantic relationships that broke up, sometimes over apparently small things. Often these men still had a very strong tie to their mother. Mom may have needed them to be a surrogate spouse or may have tried to live vicariously through their life and experience. These men need to spiritually, symbolically and then emotionally cut the ties to Mom, not as an act of rejection but as a healthy separation.

Men who have been smothered are tied tight to their mother and simultaneously carry immense anger toward her, often without even realizing it. They may express that anger toward any woman who has any expectations. The clue is the intensity of the anger. If it's rooted in the relationship with their mom, it will seem far out of proportion to the immediate cause.

Women can also feel smothered by their mother, but the way the smothering feels is often very different. Mother-daughter relationships have their own complexity. Often smothering in these relationships is expressed through intense rejection and criticism on both sides. But the healing process still involves cutting the ties and separating in a healthy way, just as it does in a smothering mother-son relationship.

IMPACT ON SEXUALITY

If Mom was not there when we needed her, we may feel rage and shame and need to have a sexual encounter whenever separation anxiety comes on. Anxious tension often locates in the genitals and so is released there. Feelings of shame are rooted in the sense of being rejected.

People also often flip into their head to try to escape feelings of pain. They may lose themselves in sexual fantasies, or they may lock into a never-ending cycle of anxious, undirected thoughts.

A sexual fantasy life may be a filler for the empty inner place left by loss of nurture. The fantasy life is a replacement attachment, not to any real relationship of nurture but to illusory experiences of the primary substitutes for nurture: adrenaline and emotional comfort.

STAGES OF SEVERITY

The severity of deprivation of a mom's nurture is reflected in the severity of the consequences. There are discernible stages of response related to the severity of the experience. You can see those stages in a baby. The first stage is protest (anger or rage). The baby cries inconsolably or rages uncontrollably.

The next stage is detachment. The baby stops crying and raging, gets quiet, lies listless, goes inward.

The final stage is attachment to another object. In extreme cases fetishism is the result. The baby, later the adult, has attached to some substitute object. In adolescence the attachment can become sexualized. The person may attach to a piece of clothing, like socks or lacy underwear, or to a body part. In either case the attachment is to something that represents the distant mom and the nurture they needed. It is safer to attach to the piece of clothing or the body part than to a real person who can remain distant and can reject you.

If you feel as if these issues connect for you but aren't sure how, you may want to look back at the symptoms of a lack of being and well-being. Because the mother is so crucial in our first ten years of life, before we experience much self-consciousness, wounds from lack of connection to our mom often run deep, beyond the reach of our self-awareness. I often pray for people who have all the symptoms of lacking a strong sense of being or well-being but are not in touch with the roots of their struggles. They don't really remember what their early experiences with their mother were like. They can think about it rationally but can't connect to their childhood feelings. Often, then, people first realize their need for healing of mother wounds by identifying with the symptoms.

It can be much easier to identify our father wounds and receive healing for them, because dads are especially important in adolescence. We were more self-aware by then, so now we can more easily connect to our feelings and experiences in that stage of life. Yet for some, issues related to connection with Mom are severe enough or have lasted so long that they are the place to start in seeking healing.

RECEIVING BEING AND WELL-BEING FROM GOD

What brings healing? God's being is weighty with reality and substance. God is the source of being. Entering into us, God gives us the reality and substance of being we lack. We receive God's presence through drinking in the Scriptures, using imagination, intuition and symbol to connect with God, and through receiving God's substance into our being by the Holy Spirit. We have Christ in us, the hope of glory. "For in him we live and move and have our being" (Acts 17:28). And the old has passed away; we are a new creation. Out of our union with Christ through the Holy Spirit we receive into our very being the being of the living, radiant God.

Remember what I emphasized earlier about the presence of God: the presence of God is the most real thing we ever encounter. To appropriately imagine God's presence, we should envision it as something *heavier* than matter.[2] It is radiant like gold, heavy like lead, molten like lava. God's presence within us gives us radiance and substance of being.[2]

God's presence is real and substantial and radiant whether we feel it or not! As Tom Trevethan writes in *The Beauty of God's Holiness*:

> As we consider what it means to live for the glory of the Holy One, it is very important to stress these twin ideas of objectivity and manifestation. The glory of God is awesomely, blindingly real, quite independent of our perception or orientation toward or against it. It's meant above all to be revealed. To live for the glory of the Lord is to act so that his glory may be manifested and made tangible. To glorify the Lord, then, is to draw attention to him, to act so that his inherent, towering majesty, authority and goodness become visible. To glorify the Lord is to think and act so that something of the pillar of cloud and fire that fell on Sinai in a blazing display of majesty will rest in perceptible reality on our lives. Clearly, this will be wonderful for us. But better still, it will point beyond us to the sheer wonder of our God.[3]

Isn't it interesting that Moses lived for forty days and forty nights without food and water, feeding only on the presence of God (Exodus 34:28)?

God's presence is the key to healing when we have a deficit related to being and well-being. God's presence is ultimately real and ultimately satisfying. For those with a shaky sense of being, as for all of us, God is the only hope.

Recognizing that God's Being is our hope, we must remember that God works incarnationally, through flesh and blood, symbol and sacrament. When we seek being and well-being, God's presence will come to us through the things that represent nurture for us. That is why it's usually helpful for women to pray the sense of being and well-being into those who long for mother nurture.

RECEIVING BEING AND WELL-BEING THROUGH PRAYER

Once again a step-by-step prayer guide for this healing is provided in the "Reflection and Response" section. You can pray through the process on your own, but it is better to move through these deep, sensitive soul issues with another who can guide and minister to you. Often after prayers for being and well-being, the best conclusion is to receive a hug from a healthy woman who can be a channel for the nurture of the living, loving God.[4]

When I pray these prayers for a man, I place one hand on his back and one hand on his chest. If I am praying for a woman, I ask her to cross her hands over her chest; then I place one hand on her hands and the other on her back. I want to pray for the sense of being and well-being to enter deeply into her heart and soul, so the placement of my hands symbolizes God's going deeply into her being where God is most needed.

When I can, I always work with a woman in this prayer, because women are incarnational channels of the nurturing, feminine love of God. In prayers like these it is very helpful to have pairs, one man and one woman, ministering together. At the end I ask my female partner to simply hold the one who has suffered and is now receiving from God. This closing embrace can be very precious. Some sufferers have never once in their life experienced holy touch and real love. In the opening story of this book, Tom experienced exactly this kind of resting in the Lord.

What lasting change is brought by the filling of the Holy Spirit for being and well-being? That is a tough question. Even after such holy and healing moments, people often experience terrifying moments of emptiness again. Sometimes then they doubt God's power to heal or decide nothing happened or seek to have the experience of being filled again and again.

I too was taken aback when I felt a return of that old unwelcome companion, separation anxiety. Not only did I experience anxiety, but now I had the new anxiety of wondering whether I had been healed and what I was doing wrong! At times I felt my last state was worse than my first.

In the end we are healed through our choices more than through any experience we receive. We are healed through listening and obedience to God. Often our sense of being and well-being grows as we minister to others, even in areas in which we feel inadequate and empty.

Experiences give us hope, energize us, break the impasse of depression and despair, give us a sense of God's care and involvement and reality. Those dimensions of the healing journey are not to be taken lightly, even after the experience fades. Sometimes cultivating a good memory is all it takes to keep us faithful and moving forward.

But we will always be tempted to choose the easier way, to look for the quick fix, to escape our pain at any price. In the end, being and well-being come from choosing to act as persons of worth who give the love that we have and minister out of the insight and gifts that God gives. It is as God is active in us and through us to heal and love others that we are healed. Jesus himself taught us that we find our lives by losing them. There is no other way. And the healing moments, when understood and harnessed rightly, can provide immense encouragement, strengthening and direction for life's long obedience and gradual becoming.

So let us give thanks to the Lord!

FOR REFLECTION AND RESPONSE

Here is a guide for prayer through the process of receiving God's nurturing and substantial presence. Again, be in a quiet place of beauty, in an atmosphere of worship. These are tender prayers, so it is best that we pursue them in a context of community, with people whom we trust.

First, focus on God's presence with you and tune your ears and heart to his voice: *Another lives in you.* That is the most important and decisive dimension of who you are and who you are becoming.

Pray John 14:19-20, 23:

Before long, the world will not see me anymore, but you will see me. Because I live, you also will live. On that day you will realize that I am in my Father, and you are in me, and I am in you. . . . If anyone loves me, he will obey my teaching. My Father will love him, and we will come to him and make our home with him.

Meditate on and affirm this. Then, from this place of faith and of listening, move to the next step of confession.

I confess any ways I have tried to find comfort apart from you and your ways. I confess the times I have used sex or food or masturbation or fed my fantasy life to escape or numb my anxiety. I confess the shame I have felt about who I am and the shame I have felt over the ways I have managed my anxiety and sought to be comforted apart from you.

Take time in God's presence to review the ways you have done this. Then pray:

Lift the shame off now, Lord. Fill those empty places with your presence, Lord.

In God's presence now express the hurt and anger you felt, perhaps unconsciously, toward your mother for the times she wasn't able to be there for you.

Let the anger or hurt come up now, Lord. It's like I am a baby crying, blue in the face, angry that I am not being loved and grieving at the loss of nurture and touch. I pray for all the repressed grief in my soul to come out, all the deep sobs of longing for attachment and comfort. Lord, I know you are here to take the hurt, the grief, the anger into yourself on the cross.

Now pray that God will give you a deep, abiding sense of true feminine love in your whole being.

May the genuine feminine love, the love of Mother, the true love you carry in your heart, Lord Jesus—may that love come into my heart. Jesus, you had a wonderful, mysterious experience of being in Mary's womb and at her breast. May you give this to me as well. May that feminine presence and peace travel into every cell of my being, peace that can come into my pelvis to release the tension.

Expand my soul now, Lord. Open my heart to receive your healing. Most important, minister the feminine into my soul. Create in me a deep pool of being. I was a dry cave. Now, Lord, pour in the waters of your nurturing presence and peace. I drink it in, thinking I will never be full. But you promise I will be full and that I will teem with life.

Finally, rest in the Lord. Keep receiving his healing work and presence.

Like a weaned child at Mother's breast is my soul. May my soul be like a weaned child at rest, cheek lying on Mother's skin.

Spend time now resting in God's presence.

12

Healing Father Wounds

Jennifer grew up in a loving home, with extended family members visiting often. She was basically a caring and fairly happy person, except in her marriage. She had started well, but several years into the marriage she began to withdraw emotionally and sexually. She felt pressured about sex and anxious every time she thought about it. She realized that while growing up she had been sexually abused a couple of times by her dad, but she had never really thought about the impact on her emotional and sexual relationships.

In her fifth year of marriage she melted down emotionally. She began thinking more and more about the experiences of abuse, and she sought counseling to help her work through the issues. The counselor was wise and understood well the powerful partnership between counseling and prayer ministry. She invited me to pray with this young woman, so we prayed for her together.

Jennifer had made real progress in understanding her struggles but had not moved ahead emotionally and sexually. So we invited her to receive prayer for the healing of memories (a topic that will be explored at length in chapter thirteen).

In an atmosphere of worship, Jennifer quieted her heart, feeling safe with her therapist and me. I asked her to bring to mind the memory of the abuse. She was able to see it with her mind's eye: she was in her room upstairs, lying down, when her father approached suddenly in the dark. It had happened before. She was frightened.

I asked her to invite Jesus into the memory. After all, God is present everywhere and was in some sense present even then. What's more, I have learned that God wants us to reframe many of our memories by inviting Jesus to give us perspective and hope. Jesus wants to be Lord of our memories, but few of us have brought our memories consciously before him.

At first Jennifer was unable to see Jesus in her mind's eye. We waited. I had an image of Jesus looking at her with compassion, and I described that. She began to sense that Jesus was present but was unable to look at him. When she did begin to picture Jesus, she saw him as Aslan, the lion in C. S. Lewis's Narnia Chronicles. At this point in her journey, she didn't feel safe seeing Jesus as a man.

I encouraged her to share her pain with Jesus, with Aslan. She began to weep and knew that Jesus was present and wept for her. As her pain poured out in Jesus' presence, her heart began to thaw. At first she was unable to grieve deeply her father's inability to give her the healthy father-love she needed. But I started to grieve on her behalf, and then she too started to weep.

After we grieved the loss for a time, I asked if she could begin to speak to her father and extend forgiveness. Unforgiveness was a cancer in her soul, making her unable to love other men and receive love. Extending forgiveness from the heart is the only path back to the freedom to love and be loved.

At first Jennifer couldn't forgive her father from her heart. But when she turned back to Aslan in her mind's eye, she was able to begin speaking to her father: she said she understood his pain and loneliness and the abuse he himself had experienced growing up, but she was hurt and angry with him. He had owed her love and blessing but had taken from her and abused her instead. Nevertheless, she chose to forgive him and to ask Jesus to forgive him. Again she began to weep.

Jennifer was coming free. Counseling had taught her to understand her problem, and now prayer was leading her into the presence of God to receive healing and begin to love and receive love again. She continued in counseling after that prayer time, and we had several more healing prayer sessions. As she extended forgiveness more and more deeply, and also received forgiveness for the destructive ways she had responded to pain, she gained strength to make new choices in her closest relationships. Healing was a long journey for Jennifer, but she had now passed some major milestones on the way.

When our father has been distant or abusive, there are many consequences. Women who were abused by their fathers may trade sexual experiences in order to feel affirmed and keep the attention of men. Many abused men and women become workaholics, addicted to influence, power and success, trying to earn their earthly father's pride and approval. Others become passive and withdrawn, without a sense of healthy gender identity. In our society, few things are more crucial then the healing of father wounds.

A healthy father blesses his children's sense of competence and gender identity. When interactions with Dad have been disordered, distant or destructive, we grow up lacking a sense of competence and security in our gender identity. The consequences are enormous.

FEAR OF AGGRESSION

Dads set boundaries.[1] When our fathers violate our boundaries, we can fear for our very life. We may feel afraid around aggressive people. Strong men push our buttons. The world around us may feel like an unsafe place.

Often, people who have experienced a father's violation of their boundaries have great difficulty building healthy relationships with men. Men may choose to relate only to women. Women may never have lasting and trusting relationships with men. I have often prayed with women who long to be married, but whenever they are in a real relationship with a real man they pull back, quickly frightened. People who have experienced violence, abuse or rage long for connection and love but find they are unable to open their heart and trust others. I have also talked with many women who reacted by marrying a "safe" man, only to find they are profoundly frustrated by his passivity and lack of strength. Only later do they realize that they married him because they were afraid of masculine strength and power.

Those who have been assaulted by rage may fear their own anger. Often people who have experienced anger and rage from their father either pour out rage indiscriminately toward others or bottle it up. These "anger bombs" usually have no idea how profoundly anger is damaging all their relationships. If they express anger in destructive ways, they may not even be aware of it. Conversely, people who bottle it up may feel like very angry people yet be unable to express even healthy anger with others. Others experience them as gentle, maybe even as a wimp.

FEAR OF FAILURE, UNHEALTHY DRIVENNESS

A healthy father affirms our sense of competence. When our capabilities have been unaffirmed, we can fear failure so much that we hold back from taking risks or expressing our true gifts. We may become passive, almost apologetic if we ever initiate. Or we may compensate for our insecurity and sense of insignificance by always trying to prove ourselves. We may be gifted, but others experience us as having an attitude, an edge, a chip on our shoulder. We may also be competitive in destructive ways, looking at others as foes to beat in the game of life. We may achieve the results we want and win the prizes but lose all the relationships that matter.

One of my greatest struggles has been drivenness. When I become driven to prove myself and force my way forward, I get off focus and out of balance. My closest relationships always pay the highest price.

GENDER CONFUSION AND INSECURITY

A healthy father affirms our gender identity.[2] If Dad was absent, distant or weak, his son may never have bonded with him or identified with him as a man. His daughter may have experienced a void rather than a blessing on her identity as a woman.

I have often prayed with women who have internalized a negative view of themselves, an image that may not reflect who they really are or how others perceive them. Recently I prayed with a stunningly beautiful woman who truly thought she was ugly. Her father had communicated that message, and she had internalized it. She had experienced a series of broken relationships with men, because she lived out of a self-fulfilling prophecy of her insignificance and unattractiveness. To see this woman's giftedness and beauty, and to learn of her terribly distorted self-image, took my breath away. It was a tragedy!

AMBIVALENCE TOWARD AUTHORITY AND POWER

A father generally represents authority and power for his children, though of course mothers can as well. So if our father was unsafe or unaffirming, we may have very complicated and conflicted relationships with other authority figures.

If you had an unsafe or unaffirming relationship with Dad, you may alternate between idolizing authority figures and turning on them when they seem to let you down. You may also find it hard to take appropriate authority over others. You may fear you will be overbearing, yet the greater risk is that you will compensate in the other direction and not provide enough boundaries.

One evidence of authority-figure ambivalence is when you put too much energy into and even obsess about what authority figures think about you. If you have this ambivalence, you may watch every move a supervisor makes and interpret every comment in relation to yourself. The authority person may just be having a bad day, but you tend to take personally every comment and every gesture. If she sends a positive message, you relax and feel good about yourself and about her. But if she sends a negative message or offers even a small criticism, or if she simply doesn't greet you in the way you would like, you start to worry. You think about how to escape the situation or how to show her that she has missed it with you.

Such constant inner questioning about what authority figures think of you can be very exhausting. It is also often exhausting for your supervisors or leaders, once they begin to realize how tuned in you are to every move they make and every word they speak.

A word of warning if you are in authority: be careful when people idolize you. The other side of the coin—anger, even rage and disillusionment—will soon appear. One mistake on your part can call it all forth. Deflect the tendency to worship you as a leader as energetically as you deflect tendencies to attack you as a leader. Paul and Barnabas certainly experienced this maddening tendency among wounded followers. One moment they were being worshiped as gods; the next moment they were lying half-dead on the street from stoning (see Acts 14)! In chapter seventeen we will look further at transference of feelings from past experiences onto present relationships.

IMPACT ON SEXUALITY

For men, homosexual attraction is often rooted in Dad's absence, distance or rejection. Homosexual strugglers have often not bonded to their father or come into a sense of their own masculinity. So they look to others who have what they are missing. Sexual union between men is often an attempt to become one with what we lack and to fill our inner emptiness.

Some male homosexual couples include a more "feminine" and a more "masculine" partner. Often homosexual strugglers are trying to connect with the unaffirmed side of their personality. The more "masculine" guy feels unaffirmed in the feminine side, and he bonds with that unaffirmed self through sex with another man. The true need is not for sex with someone who represents the unaffirmed part of us, but rather for learning to affirm and embrace that part in healthier, more self-aware ways.

Of course there are many other ways we react to being unaffirmed in our gender identity. Some men, maybe especially men who were belittled by Dad, have a violent side to sexual relationships. Even pornography can be a means of feeling powerful. But once again, the sense of significance and potency that comes from using pornography is illusory. It doesn't last or develop into inner strength.

For women, distance, rejection or abuse by Dad can lead to a rejection of all men and the pursuit of lesbianism. Many women have chosen to become sexually intimate with other women because they were violated through sexual abuse and feel they could never trust men.

But Dad's distance or rejection can also lead to a woman's unhealthy dependency on men. I have prayed, along with a woman cominister, for many women who gave themselves away sexually because they needed male affirmation, were afraid of losing a relationship, felt pressure to have sex and didn't have enough sense of worth to be able to say no. Sometimes the shame surrounding such past choices is far more debilitating than the choice itself. Choices to violate our inner sense of right and wrong, our personal integrity, break down the walls of our personality. I have prayed for many who felt distance or disapproval from Dad, had sex with a boyfriend, and then lived for years in painful shame about who they are and what they have done; they are not sure they can ever be loved or valued again.

Finally, men who are unaffirmed may seek the affirmation they need from women, through sexual experiences or in other ways. But the affirmation never really satisfies. A woman may feel like a safer person with whom to seek a sense of potency and affirmation, but when the deficit is in the area of a father's blessing, affirmation from women will never be enough.

STAGES OF SEVERITY

Once again, there are different stages of severity in the ways we responded to our father's lack of blessing of our gender identity and competency. At first a teen may be defensive, angry and rebellious toward Dad and other authority figures. In the next stage, there is an escape away or a turn inward into fantasy, depression and passivity. We feel inadequate, impotent, depressed. Finally, as anger and self-hatred build up, abuse may turn outward against others or ourselves, ending in violence or suicide.

HOW DO WE RECEIVE A FATHER'S BLESSING THROUGH PRAYER?

God is the true Father who blesses!

Think of Jesus at his baptism. At that point he had not yet launched his public ministry: he had accomplished nothing and influenced no one that we know about. But he received the Father's blessing at the beginning, not just at the end of his ministry. He was the Beloved of God,[3] and he knew it, not because of his accomplishments but because of his identity as God's Son.[4]

In our own baptism we enter into union with Christ. We become sons and daughters of God. We are God's Beloved, blessed because of our relationship with God and not because of our performance. Just as Jesus did, we hear the Father's voice in our baptism: "This is my beloved son, my beloved daughter, in whom I am well pleased." God is speaking this word to all of us. He began to speak this word at our baptism. We are his Beloved; we belong to him. He is proud of us, not because of our performance but because of our relationship, our identity, our identification with Jesus.

God sees our real self and blesses us. We can hear God's true word to us, God's pride in us and blessing on us. We can live on the foundation of already being beloved, blessed in our gender identity, our giftedness and our potential for competency. We do not have to earn those things or prove anything to anybody. Our real self is not our addictive self, our dependent self, our raging self or our despairing self. Those identities were not created by God or blessed by God, nor ultimately will they be redeemed by God. We can learn to rest in God's word to us about who we truly are, God's blessing on our true identity, belovedness and giftedness.

But how do we learn to hear God's word to us about our belovedness? How do we receive God's blessing and believe it in our heart, especially if we have heard contradictory words from our earthly father? I have found that before people receive into their souls the blessing of God as Father, they need to work through hard issues of forgiveness. Unforgiveness blocks our ability to receive blessing and acceptance. The healing of memories may be the most helpful step we can take toward receiving God's blessing into our hearts.

We will look next at this healing of our memories. Then we will explore some prayers for the healing of father wounds.

FOR REFLECTION AND RESPONSE

1. What symptoms of the lack of a father's blessing can you identify with?

2. To what degree are you able to rest in being God's beloved and blessed son or daughter, merely by virtue of your identity and identification with Jesus?

3. What healthy man can you think of who might be able to work through this chapter with you and pray for you?

Forgiveness and Healing Memories

Early in this book I told how I had gone to bed one night with the haunting image of a man I had known when I was younger coming at me full of rage, holding a knife. The next day I was praying with my friend William; he saw the same image when we went to pray, even though I had not mentioned the experience to anyone. I then told him about the image and the real-life experience I'd had with that man. In his understated way, William expressed the thought that maybe God wanted us to pray about this man with the dagger.

As we began to pray, William directed me to bring the image up again on the screen of my mind's eye. I did. William then encouraged me to invite Jesus to come into the image and express his love and lordship. I saw with my mind's eye Jesus entering the picture, walking up to the man, grabbing the knife out of his hand and pushing him away from me. He didn't hurt the man. He just stopped him cold. Then he spoke: "You take your hands off my beloved son!" The man slunk away.

Jesus turned toward me and spoke these words: "You are my beloved child. You are special to me." Then he picked me up and cradled me.

As the scene began, I was an adolescent, as I had been when I encountered the man. That actual encounter had not included a knife, but it had coalesced my fear of overwhelming masculine strength, anger and energy, expressed graphically in my imagination as the man coming at me with a knife.

Then when Jesus cradled me, I was suddenly three, and he was speaking to that anxious part of me that needed a sense of well-being.

Of course this healing would have been very encouraging to me if it had ended there. But William was wiser than to let me merely bask in the new heart sense that Jesus loved and protected me. I hadn't yet taken some crucial steps for healing. So William next directed me to forgive the man I had felt attacked by. I could have said the words "I forgive you" easily, but first I needed to remember and even reexperience the hurt and rejection and woundedness I felt. I entered back into the memory and started expressing my feelings of hurt, anger and sadness at the emotional abuse I had received. Then, empowered by the sense of being loved and protected by Jesus, I was able to extend forgiveness from the heart. I pictured the man and now said much more genuinely than I ever had before, "I forgive you." A great weight lifted off my heart. I also asked Jesus to forgive this man.

Forgiving others is progressive, like peeling the layers off an onion. The deeper we enter into our pain and loss, and then the more profoundly God speaks truth and healing into those places of pain and loss, the more fully we let go of the debt owed us and so are healed. We forgive not only with our mind but more deeply from our heart.

After extending forgiveness, I needed to go on to *ask* forgiveness for the defensive and self-protective patterns of behavior I had developed in response to the way I had been sinned against. I confessed my fear in relationships, my drivenness to prove myself, and my repression and fear of my own anger.

William blessed these prayers of extending and receiving forgiveness. My heart melted, and for the first time I felt truly free from the effects of my experience with the harsh man. I felt free to love, be more openhearted, rest in being accepted and blessed without proving myself. I cannot overstate how profound a breakthrough this event was. I began to see how forgiveness lies at the heart of most true healing.

Here is the healing of memories in a nutshell: Jesus exercises his lordship and healing presence in our memories and mental images, giving us strength to extend and receive forgiveness for the ways we have been sinned against and the ways we have sinned in response.

Jesus can enter into our memories through our imagination and exert his lordship. In some sectors of the church we have been very committed to bringing every *thought* under the lordship of Christ. But we have often left our imagination and memories to run their course, independent of what Jesus might want to do and say to us about them. Jesus is to be Lord of our imagination and of our memories. Jesus wants to sanctify or cleanse and claim our imagination and memories. Have you heard me say that before? I hope so!

HEALING AND TRUTH

Now by healing our memories Jesus doesn't change what happened to us in the past. Healing will always involve telling the truth about who we are and what has happened. One of the greatest barriers to healing is our inability to face what actually happened, to name events and people for what they did and what they are. If we have experienced evil, we *must* face it and name it for what it is. At times I have prayed for a person who grew up in an atmosphere of unspeakable evil. One crucial step in their healing is for them to admit it, to call what is evil by its true name. But even if what we experienced was more typical, not so horrendous, the path of healing still runs through the gateway of telling the truth about it.

If we were sinned against, we will need to face that reality and be able to describe it, and often even feel it, before we can receive God's healing. Trying to extend forgiveness to those who have sinned against us before we have fully grasped and named the harm they did often results in a superficial forgiveness that comes from our head, not our heart. If we have forgiven only superficially, we often continue to carry deep wounds and unresolved hurt and anger. I believe the church is full to the brim with such superficial forgiveness. Forgiveness must go deeper and become more genuine if our relationships, including our relationship to God, are to truly be healed. Healing memories is a wonderful gift of the Spirit to help us fully appropriate and apply the power of forgiveness.

If we sinned in response to sins done against us, we will need to be able to admit that, describe the ways we sinned, and even feel the harm we caused to ourselves and others before we can receive healing. The path of healing always travels through the gateway of truth.

I have often prayed with people who will not or can not tell the truth about their past. They justify horrifying sins of abuse or violence against them when they were very young. They excuse their parents and other adults who did such things. We are called to honor our parents, but honoring our parents and facing reality go together. We honor our parents rightly by affirming the good things they gave us and also by pursuing healing and full forgiveness for any sins and even evil that we experienced.

The path of healing, and for that matter, honoring others rightly, always leads through the gateway of truth.

So what does the healing of memories actually accomplish?

Many of the false words about who we are and how unlovable, incompetent, ungifted and unattractive we are have been wrapped up in our negative experiences with others, particularly with parents.

We receive and believe words about our identity and potential that are limiting and destructive. I have prayed with artistically gifted men whose father thought the arts were "sissy stuff," too feminine. Their fundamental giftedness and contribution to the world lie under a cloud from that false word. I have prayed with women who were "supposed" to be a son, and knew it, and knew that as a daughter they would never be able to measure up or be loved. In certain cultures, and our own as well, the sin of *misogyny,* the hatred of women, is common and profoundly destructive.

Many people have perfectionist parents for whom they could never do enough, never be good enough. A critical spirit was turned upon everything they ever did. This critical spirit is often internalized, a voice that speaks in their head every time they start to feel insecure, inadequate or under stress.

Those negative words that have lodged in our heart, often connected to memories of especially destructive experiences, must be replaced by words, experiences and memories that speak the truth about who we are and lodge this truth in our heart.

Jesus must be Lord not only of what we think about ourselves consciously but also of how we see ourselves, feel about ourselves, imagine ourselves unconsciously. This healing of our inner image is crucial for us to learn to live in our belovedness and our blessedness in God.

So we bring to our mind's eye the experiences, images and memories that generated false words about who we are, and we invite Jesus into them. He can exert his lordship over our memories and inner images to sanctify and heal us. He doesn't change the experiences and memories, but he does speak the truth about who God is, who we are and how God names us. In addition, God can give us insight into the ways Jesus was protecting us even in the most difficult experiences of our lives.

God can even reach unconscious memories through the healing of memories. For instance, I once prayed for a young woman who knew she had been in an incubator for a month in infancy but had no conscious memory of that time. She invited Jesus into that unconscious memory and began to see with the eyes of her heart how Jesus was present to her. Asking Jesus into that memory and seeing that he was there put her in touch with the deep loss she suffered as a baby but also a deep sense of being loved and held by Jesus. This healing had a profound impact on her. She was now able to connect to the loss and extend forgiveness toward her parents and doctors, though she understood that parents and doctors at that time didn't know the effects of isolating a baby from human touch and parents' voices.

As I said in an earlier chapter, images and symbols are the bridge between thoughts and feelings, particularly in relation to things we can't see. This is true for how we imagine God, but also for the ways we imagine ourselves and our soul.

We can't see our self-image. We can't see our own soul. So the symbols and images of personhood, of masculinity, of femininity and of our selves that we carry within, rooted in our experiences, go a long way toward determining the health of our soul. To heal our self-image, we must receive healing of the images and memories that helped define it.

In addition to healing our image of ourselves, an even more crucial element is really the primary function of the healing of memories. *The healing of memories is for the forgiveness of sins.*[1] Memories are healed when they are robbed of their power to lead us into sin or to internalize the damage of sins done against us.

Some prayer ministers use the healing of memories primarily to give people affirming experiences of hearing from God. They use the healing of memories *therapeutically* but fall short of the biblical call to the cure of souls. The affirming experiences are good, but they are meant to serve God's intention to cleanse and change us through the forgiveness of sins.

SINNERS AND SINNED AGAINST

All of us are sinners. And all of us have been sinned against. That's reality. And these two facts about us are often deeply connected to one another. Often our most enduring and destructive sinful patterns come out of the ways we have responded to being sinned against. Violence begets violence. When we have been belittled or abused, we often become abusers and feel little control over our behavior. Experiences of rejection beget shame, and shame often leads to acting out sexually. Lack of parental nurture and blessing can leave tremendous holes in our soul, holes that we often choose to fill in self-destructive ways. In these cases and many others, our most enduring and destructive sins are rooted in our response to being sinned against. We are still responsible, even though others have had a part by sinning against us.

The solution for sin is always the same: we repent of our sins, and we forgive those who sinned against us. Forgiveness means we let go of the debt we were owed, in this case by parents.

Nothing is more crucial for healing than forgiveness. Nothing.

As Paul tells us, we leave retribution to God. Ultimately we know there will be justice. But it is not our place to mete it out, especially in our personal relationships. Our part is to let go of the debt we were owed, whether a debt of love, nurture, affirmation or protection, and learn to walk in freedom from the destructive things done against us and the destructive things we have done. In the end we are healed when we can love and long for the best for those who have hurt us. Then we have become truly free.

The healing of memories helps us receive with our heart what we have always known with our head as Christians. We know we're forgiven, but we don't receive it into our heart. We know we are to forgive, but we don't forgive from our heart. The imagination is the bridge between the head and the heart.

We extend forgiveness for the ways we have been sinned against.

Forgiving someone is not the same thing as acting as if the wrong didn't happen. Forgiveness is assigning moral responsibility for what happened and expressing to God our hurt and anger. Then by an act of the will, empowered by Jesus, we choose to let go of the debt that is owed us. This act of forgiveness often becomes heartfelt and deep when we have connected the hurt we feel with particular experiences and memories.

As we grow more mature and go deeper with God and others, we uncover new dimensions of our need to forgive and be forgiven. Forgiveness, then, is a process with crucial moments along the way.

Throughout that process, Jesus can come into any memory or image. Jesus is Lord of our images, our memories and all of who we are.

How does the healing of memories work? What are the steps?

The process is actually quite simple. We bring to mind—or let God bring to mind—painful experiences or memories, or images connected to those experiences and memories. We then invite Jesus to enter the memory or image and give Jesus the freedom to show us his lordship and love. Sometimes we see nothing happen, and that's okay. At other times, Jesus acts before our mind's eye in a way we might have expected. But sometimes Jesus does the unexpected, and these times often prove to be quite powerful.

As we respond to what Jesus does, our heart is encouraged, and the false words we have heard about ourselves are replaced with God's true word. Then we can feel the pain of the loss, the hurt of not receiving what we were owed. We face and feel the pain of being sinned against. From that place, facing the pain while feeling encouraged and strengthened, and out of sensing that we are the beloved, we now have a greater capacity to forgive from our heart. We forgive the sins against us, however terrible, and come out from being controlled by their effects. Then we are freer to see the sinful ways we responded and to take responsibility for them. We ask forgiveness and receive cleansing and strengthening to make new choices and believe new words about ourselves. Now our prayer to be delivered from evil and the effects of evil has new meaning and power.

Lewis Smedes's description of the process of forgiveness in his *Forgive and Forget* is helpful: we hurt, we hate, we heal and we come together.[2] Forgiveness that too quickly passes over the hurting and hating stages will often have to be revisited.

The healing of memories can be a profoundly life-giving process. Let's walk through it together in prayer.

FOR REFLECTION AND RESPONSE

The moments in which Jesus enters and assumes lordship over memories and our imagination are tender and important. This prayer exercise will lead you toward healing through forgiving your parents. You will need to be quiet, in a safe, beautiful and worshipful space, and it will help to be with people who can help you through any places where you might get stuck.

First, practice God's presence and tune your ears and your heart to his voice. Another lives in you. That is the most decisive dimension of who you are and who you are becoming.

Pray John 14:19-23:

Before long, the world will not see me anymore, but you will see me. Because I live, you also will live. On that day you will realize that I am in my Father, and you are in me, and I am in you. . . . If anyone loves me, he will obey my teaching. My Father will love him, and we will come to him and make our home with him.

Pray and affirm this. Stay in this place of listening.

In prayer, see Jesus towering over your parents. Jesus is greater than them, greater than any problem you face. As I've prayed with others, I have often found that when they imagine their parents at this precious moment, their parents look huge and they see themselves as very small. So I ask them to invite Jesus in. I ask Jesus to show them how big he is. Often they will realize Jesus is huge next to their parents. That image can be a beginning of putting parents in perspective.

Receive Jesus' presence, true word and power to forgive into the unaffirmed places in your soul. By speaking his redemptive, healing, affirming word, Jesus begins to deliver you from the destructive power of that person who has harmed you.

Invite Jesus into any disturbing memory or experience. With the eyes of your heart, see his love and care for you, his ability to empower you to forgive those who have hurt you.

God can minister to memories that are conscious, but God can even reach back into memories from the womb or early years to which we have no conscious access. I have often prayed for people who had a profound dis-ease and anxiety about early years or even birth, but no conscious memories of what happened. We can invite Jesus to enter into the memories locked in our unconscious. Jesus wants to be Lord even of these memories.

When you invite Jesus into a memory or image, get in a relaxed position and be open to whatever Jesus might want to say or do.

You may find that images and pictures come quite slowly. This is not surprising: you are not used to letting God work in this part of yourself. Give it time. Do what you can to maintain a receptive, openhearted spirit. Sometimes I like to walk in the woods, worship, and receive God's presence and peace before I invite God to work through images and within memories.

One mistake people often make: as soon as they start to see Jesus, they wonder if it's real or if they are just making it up. Here once again we meet the disease of introspection, where we turn our critical, skeptical faculties on our intuitive perceptions and freeze them out. Don't do that. Suspend your critical faculty for a time. There will be plenty of time later to reflect on, assess and critique your experience. As the late Clyde Kilby, professor of literature at Wheaton College and a C. S. Lewis scholar, used to say, "Fellows, you can't kiss your girl and think about it at the same time." The attempt to do them simultaneously robs the experience of its power and the analysis of its basis in meaningful experience.

In prayer, express the pain and anger you felt, and then choose to forgive, to let go of the debt owed you. You can never have back what has been lost. You can never be three or eight or thirteen again. Letting go of the debt frees you to receive what God and others are giving, allows you to build the relationship that *is* possible, and frees the person who sinned against you from your demands and accusations.

When we do not forgive, we let the person who sinned against us control our life. When we do forgive and let go of the debt they owed us, we are free to let God lead our life.

But forgiveness from the heart happens only as we feel the pain, assign moral responsibility and let go of the debt with dignity. You are a person of worth; you should have been treated better. As Bill Leslie, the pastor who launched me into healing ministry, said, "Rick, you are worth getting angry over." Only after you have experienced and expressed the anger you feel when you're healthy enough to value yourself appropriately can you forgive from the heart.

Too often "forgiving" is actually acquiescing to abuse. In essence, we say, "I forgive you. I wasn't really worth better treatment anyway." That is the opposite of true forgiveness. That posture is merely the internalization of false words and of self-hatred.

In prayer, confess the sinful ways you responded. Have you met anger with anger, rage with rage? Have you internalized false words about yourself and fallen into depression or self-hatred? Have you tried to fill up the deficit by pursuing addictive sexual or emotional relationships or experiences? Have you been driven to achieve and acquire in order to earn love or be safe? How did you sin in response to the ways you were sinned against? How were you responsible? Can you confess and repent of those behaviors, patterns and ways of thinking? Or must you hold on to them out of fear that without those responses you won't be safe, or you won't know who you are? Can you give God your fears, confess your sins and begin to embrace the true words about who you are?

In prayer, lift off the chains that have bound you, the effects of the evil done against you. Jesus taught us to pray for deliverance from evil (or the evil one, depending on your translation of the Lord's Prayer). We can pray for God to lift off the self-fulfilling prophecies, the destructive patterns, the despair and the addictions. God can deliver us from evil and from bondage to the past.

By the Spirit, receive the fatherly blessing or motherly hug through the laying on of hands. Just being in the presence of a healthy Christian man or woman can bring healing. Healing comes through the blessings we give to one another. Later in this book we will explore how physical touch and the sacraments can be channels of healing. At the core our faith is incarnational, the unseen God taking on human flesh and blood to bless, heal and redeem God's creation. For now, just realize how powerful a healthy Christian touch can be in mediating the blessing of God to your suffering soul.

Through the embrace of truth, the exercise of your will, and the loving help and accountability of others, you can now make new choices and so be transformed, in collaboration with God's Spirit. The healing of memories helps create the possibility for new choices. But it is your choice to live based on who God is and who you truly are that sets healing into your soul in a lasting way. As I have often noted, healing experiences guarantee nothing. We become our real selves as we listen to God and obey and live in reality and community.

Battling Sexual Addiction

Bob approached me at a conference and asked if he could confess his sins to me before God. I had encouraged people who felt stuck and unforgiven to confess their sins to a trusted person who could assure them of God's forgiveness. The biblical writer James encourages us to confess our sins to church elders and to one another, and God will forgive and heal us (James 5:14-16). If we are holding on to shame and stuck in our healing journey, we need to confess our sin and shame before God and with others, and Bob was taking steps to do that.

Bob began confessing his sexual addictions to pornography on the Internet, pornographic videos and "gentlemen's clubs." He felt trapped and defeated in the cycle of shame, self-hatred, comfort and acting out that is often associated with addiction. As we prayed, I sensed that Bob was being oppressed by demonic presences related to sexual addiction.

Scripture has a lot to say about spiritual presences that are good (angels) and evil (demons and Satan). Even if we are Christian, demonic presences can influence us when we invite them to through sinful choices. These demonic influences latch onto our emotional wounds and vulnerabilities. Jesus shows us, and Scripture teaches us, that Christ has set us free, and we can walk in that freedom by exercising our authority in Christ. But "casting out" demons without attending to emotional wounds and sexual vulnerabilities is a mistake. If we are not also receiving healing of our wounds, we will just invite the influence of these presences back in later.

Bob had already received prayer for being and well-being and for strengthening of his will. He had walked through prayers for cleansing the imagination. It was now time for him to claim freedom from demonic influences. We invited God's Spirit to be present, we exalted and worshiped God for a time, and then we invited God to show us the demonic influence in Bob's life so that we might deal with it.

I directed Bob to renounce the demons and idols of sexual sin and immorality. He did so. He claimed his authority in Christ to be free of those influences. He reaffirmed Jesus as Lord. God also led him to confess and renounce his older brother's influence in leading him into pornography.

I prayed that the holy fire of God's presence would fall on Bob and consume the images and presences in his life. By this point Bob was trembling and receiving much from the touch of God. I symbolized God's cleansing by wiping water on his forehead, hands, eyelids and even lips. He was smiling by then, full of the joy of having admitted the truth, affirmed Jesus as Lord and received great cleansing and freedom.

Gabriela experienced a related healing, both from sexual addiction and from self-hatred and depression. In her growing-up years she had experienced sexual abuse. She had hated being touched intrusively, but she also longed for sexual experiences, because the moments of abuse were the only times she had felt any affection from the men in her life.

In a healing prayer small group, Gabriela prayed through a renunciation of sexual idolatry and immorality just as Bob did. But Gabriela needed more. She told us, "I can't sleep at night lately. Every time I go to bed, I feel anxious and depressed, lie awake for a couple hours, and then have nightmares when I do sleep."

We began to pray for her. Brad saw an image of Jesus taking her hand. I had a sense that Jesus took her hand because he wanted to speak to her and tell her she would not be abandoned. I asked her if there had been a time in her life when she felt abandoned.

"Yes," she responded. "When I was six, I lived with relatives who abused me emotionally and sexually. After they did it, they would lock me in my room. I was so alone."

We ministered to Gabriela over the next hour, speaking words of Jesus' grief over her experience. She invited Jesus into the memories, and he comforted her. But we sensed that she struggled with spirits of suicide, depression and self-hatred, so we directed her to renounce those. I will never forget her next prayer, because it surprised me.

"Lord," she began with a faltering voice and tears in her eyes, "I hurt so much at those times. I was so afraid of being alone. And I didn't have any sense that you were in my life. I felt like you had abandoned me. And so I turned to these spirits, these presences, of suicide, depression and self-hatred for companionship, so I wouldn't be so alone. I made friends with them because I needed something at that moment. But today I renounce that friendship. I belong to Jesus Christ. And you spirits have no right to be in my life. Be gone! Come and fill me with your love, Jesus. I need you so much. Thank you for making yourself so real in my life at this moment."

Having invited these presences into her life, Gabriela needed to take her place in Christ and disinvite them! Her experience clearly shows how Christians can be oppressed by spirits by consciously or unconsciously inviting them in. But Gabriela learned that she had the authority to tell them to leave. Deliverance is often not a dramatic confrontation between Jesus and demons but a simple act of a Jesus-follower taking his place in Christ and claiming the freedom and the authority God has already given.

The final prayer we led Gabriela in was a renunciation of the misogyny, or hatred of women, that had come to her through her family. Often sins and spirits of sexual addiction are connected to sins and spirits of the hatred of women. Many cultures, including Gabriela's, are particularly marked by a generational sin of misogyny. I'll unpack that a bit more as we journey together through this chapter.

Many people are locked in some form of sexual addiction—pornography, heterosexual or homosexual promiscuity, pedophilia or any number of other practices. In addiction there is almost always a demonic spiritual dimension that must be addressed. In my years with the Pastoral Care Ministry of Leanne Payne, we would enter into a battle with sexual addiction and its demonic dimension toward the end of our week-long conferences. We saw many miraculous interventions of God in the lives of people who were enslaved to sinful practices, thoughts and habits. The way we pursued deliverance from oppressive demonic influence and sexual idolatry is not the only way to gain this freedom in Christ. But the "Baal and Ashtoreth" prayer sessions at the Pastoral Care Ministry conferences can help illuminate the problem and the remedy.

An Evening of Deliverance

On the evening set aside for deliverance prayers, we prayer ministers were excited and anxious, wondering how it would all go. Leanne rose to teach on Baal and Ashtoreth worship as it was practiced in Old Testament times. Baal was the god of sexual fertility, and Ashtoreth was the feminine aspect of the same god. Baal had the form of a totem pole, a phallic image. Ancient peoples would gather to worship the Baals and participate in sexual immorality and orgies. Sometimes the worship of Baal would transmute into the worship of Molech, and children would be sacrificed. The sexual gods and goddesses were hungry, never satisfied. They ultimately wanted to feed not just on sexual orgy but on violence. They were hungry to feed on life itself, not just the procreative energy and faculty of life.

In the end, when people no longer worship God, they will worship the procreative force,[1] which may be the most powerful human force. That force in us transcends us. It is our creative life force, a way we humans resemble the divine Creator of life, giving birth and creation to new beings. So worship often turns to the phallic. Certainly ancient peoples worshiped the phallic as a symbol for fertility and life. But in the modern world after the Enlightenment, we have also tended to worship the procreative force, this most powerful, transcendent part of our humanity. So it happened with Sigmund Freud, who became obsessed with libido and the transmutation of sex and sexuality into all the other human drives. And in another way, it happened with Carl Jung. Jung focused on the other aspect of God, God's other face, the hidden or underground God, what Jung called the chthonic god. This hidden aspect of God for Jung was also phallic.

In our deliverance service, Leanne spoke a prophetic word she had received early in her ministry, after she had spent a long day ministering to sexually broken people, especially homosexual strugglers. Weary and exhausted, she wanted to give up for a while, to withdraw. But as she prayed, God impressed on her spirit that the battle today is the ancient battle in new guise, the battle against the Baals and Ashtoreths, the sexual gods and goddesses of fertility. These gods and goddesses are still alive and well and pervasively influencing our culture. They have an invisible dimension, a reality of being. They have been invited into human affairs on a vast scale: in the media, in movies, through advertising, through the Internet and through political leaders plagued with scandal. Everywhere these demonic powers have been invited to rule and enslave.

Our culture is returning to paganism on a vast scale. Paganism is pantheistic, seeing God present throughout creation but no longer above us with the right to rule us. Wiccan practices are becoming widespread. Sexual boundaries are disappearing. People are worshiping gods that emerge out of their own consciousness and spirituality. *The Da Vinci Code* has popularized a reinterpretation of Christian faith that arises out of pagan ideas more than Christian ideas. As a culture we have lost any transcendent reference point for values, so each of us is reduced to generating our values out of our own experiences and instincts. Each group or tribe defines its own values and truths. In the midst of such confusion over the source of values, is it any wonder that we are battling sexual dynamics, brokenness and chaos that often feels overwhelming and irreversible?

Our battle is not just against flesh and blood. Change will not happen solely through the exercise of our will, especially in our sexuality. As Paul expresses it: "For our struggle is not against flesh and blood, but against the rulers, against the authorities, against the powers of this dark world and against the spiritual forces of evil in the heavenly realms" (Ephesians 6:12). We battle larger forces, earthly and heavenly. We are enslaved to larger forces. There is a demonic dimension to our most basic struggles. And that demonic dimension must be addressed and engaged with.

So next at our healing meeting Leanne invited God's presence. She never stayed focused on demons or on principalities and powers, Paul's name for the larger forces that rule and enslave us. Only through practicing God's presence and fullness, reality and rule, are we ready to repent and renounce and be delivered and cleansed. Prayers that constantly address Satan and demons are often more an exercise in grandiosity than a real spiritual engagement and victory. Jesus is the One who battles and defeats those larger forces. It is not our verbal aggression in prayer but Jesus' cross and resurrection that bring the victory. We come into victory not by taking on Satan and demons but by inviting in the fiery, holy, all-consuming presence of the living God.

So we worshiped and prayed in that great gathering. And we waited for the tangible presence of the mighty Lord, who fights and wins the battle. At the appropriate moment, Leanne called for manifestation of the demonic presences that had been keeping people in bondage. Because of what we have done, these demons have had a right to be in our life. They often wreak havoc with our life, though we ignore them. But now the time of deliverance was at hand. God's power to confront and cast out was present.

Suddenly, all over the crowd, people began to weep, to cry out, to experience manifestations of demonic presences that had been busy but hidden. Phallic and sexual images cascaded through people's minds. Images that had obsessed them became present again in their mind's eye.

Then Leanne invoked the holy presence of God to be poured out, to wash through us like fire from heaven, to cleanse and to heal. At that moment many felt the tangible presence of God, his holy presence, the manifesting of his glory.

The glory of God fell on us, the people of God! Leanne then sent us prayer ministers through the crowd to sprinkle water that had been blessed (more on blessed water in the next chapter). As the water drops fell gently on people, you could see many tremble. Many people later told us that at that point they felt delivered and cleansed, some for the first time in their adult life.

Leanne invited people to come forward to be washed with more of the water that we had blessed in prayer. And she invited people to receive more prayer individually.

As many came forward, a woman began to wail from deep in her being. She was experiencing a related healing, healing from a self-hatred that is rooted in the hatred of women that always comes with worship of the Baals and Ashtoreths. In highly sexualized cultures, women become objects. In homosexualized cultures, at least for men, women become unnecessary. Sexual orgy destroys the honor of women. It also debases men, but women more often internalize a destructive self-hatred.

In our culture that rightfully seeks to overcome sexism, it is ironic that so many women have so much self-hatred. Is that all due to conservative, patriarchal institutions in our culture's past, like the church? Or is hatred of women endemic to many highly sexualized and highly paganized cultures? As Jewish writer Dennis Prager has it:

> Human nature, undisciplined by values, will allow sex to dominate personal lives and the life of society. When Judaism demanded that all sexual intercourse be channeled into marriage, it changed the world. It is not overstated to say that the Torah's prohibition of non-marital sex made the creation of Western civilization possible. This revolutionary channeling of sex ensured that sex would no longer dominate society, it heightened male-female love and sexuality, and it began the arduous task of elevating the status of women.
>
> Human sexuality, especially male sexuality, is utterly wild. Among the consequences of the unchanneled sex drive is the sexualization of everything. Thus, the first thing Judaism did was to desexualize God. This was an utterly radical break with

all religion, and it alone changed human history. The gods of virtually all other ancient societies engaged in sexual relations. In Judaism, sexuality would no longer dominate society.

It was Judaism alone, and then later Christianity, that about 3000 years ago declared homosexual activity wrong . . . in the most powerful and unambiguous language. Do we really want a return to the freer, more expressive and sexually chaotic pagan cultures of old? Will the sexualization of everything in our culture, and the free and unchanneled expression of our sexuality, really lead us as a culture to a desirable end?[2]

In other words, the Baals and Ashtoreths are alive and well and ruling in our day. Our culture is repaganizing! Yet current approaches to healing and life change often ignore the invisible demonic aspects of the rule of these ancient gods. Then our approaches are inadequate and often ineffective, resulting in very little lasting healing and transformation.

As we prayer ministers went through the crowd sprinkling blessed water, people were profoundly affected. Many were delivered at that point. Later on Leanne made an intriguing comment. She said, "We are finishing the work of baptism at these sessions." What she meant is that at their baptism most people had only confessed sin; they had not named and renounced ruling principalities and powers, for instance the Baals and Ashtoreths. (If the biblical names throw you off, you can use English versions, like "gods of sexual orgy and immorality." But there is something quite powerful about using the ancient names from Old Testament days.) Many at our conferences had not renounced Satan and all his works and the world and all its ways when they were baptized. Years before, many of these strugglers had prayed a salvation prayer and been baptized for repentance and the forgiveness of sins. But now they were entering intentionally into the victory of Christ over the ruling forces and beings that had enslaved them. They were entering into their baptism as a rite of exorcism. The gospel message was finally getting at the crucial part of their life, with dramatic impact.

BAPTISM AS DELIVERANCE

The early church understood baptism as identification with Jesus in his dying and rising. See Paul's discussion of it in Romans 6, where sin is treated as an enslaving power. (In some church circles we tend to see sin as just individual human attitudes and actions.) Baptism meant dying to Satan, the ways of the world and the sins of the flesh. And it meant rising to the new life in union with Christ. Baptism was not just about cleansing for individual sins. Baptism was also about the spiritual battle with Satan and the ways of the world.

Reflect on the baptismal liturgy of a modern-day church, a liturgy whose roots go all the way back to the very early centuries of the Christian church:

Do you renounce Satan and all the spiritual forces of wickedness that rebel against God?
I renounce them.
Do you renounce the evil powers of this world which corrupt and destroy the creatures of God?
I renounce them.
Do you renounce all sinful desires that draw you from the love of God?
I renounce them.
Do you turn to Jesus Christ and accept him as your Savior?
I do.
Do you put your whole trust in his grace and love?

I do.

Do you promise to follow and obey him as your Lord?

I do.[3]

Now that's a salvation prayer!

Compare that prayer to the one some of us have often used to guide others toward salvation:

I admit I have sinned, Lord. I accept Jesus' death on the cross as the payment for my sin. And I commit myself to you as my Savior and Lord.

Do you see the difference?

At conversion we were meant to *renounce* the works of Satan, the ways of the world and the sins of the flesh. In some understandings of Christian conversion we focus solely on *repenting of* the sins of the flesh. Satan and his works and the world and its ways are left out of the picture. At the conference we were completing the work of baptism, then, because we were calling people into the freedom in Christ that comes from renouncing Satan and his works and claiming Christ's victory over all that would enslave us.

There is another very important aspect to the Pastoral Care Ministries evening of deliverance and healing. We held this service late in the conference. Leanne and others had already taught about gender identity, about healthy masculinity and femininity. She had taught about how to come into a sense of being and well-being and how to receive strengthening for wills weakened by addictive habits and patterns. We had learned about how to be cleansed and set apart to God in our imaginative faculties and about how to practice God's presence and stay focused on his goodness and glory moment by moment. There was a secure basis for exorcism because there had been good teaching and ministry about personhood, gender, God and his glory, and the seamless interconnectedness of emotional, physical, spiritual and social dimensions of life. Good psychology and good spirituality are complementary in a ministry of true healing. Deliverance was not a quick fix for addiction. We had looked at the roots of addiction in our choices, our family systems and our social context. So we were ready to be delivered from demonic influence and then *stay* delivered.

There is immense jubilation in seeing people beginning to become who they were created to be before your very eyes. To see the real person shine through is wondrous. And to see the idolatries that have distorted the personality get named and renounced is powerful and profound. To reiterate C. S. Lewis's memorable words from *Till We Have Faces,* "How can we speak to God face to face, until we have faces?" That is, until the real person emerges and gains substance and actuality of being. What an immense privilege it is to see people who have been gripped by shame and enslaved by addiction speak to God face to face and receive energy and insight to choose the good, to choose life.

I invite you now to renounce sexual idolatry and the influence of those ancient gods and goddesses of fertility and orgy, the Baals and Ashtoreths. You can ask God to begin to prepare your heart for such deliverance. And you can ask God to lead you to the right place and time for these prayers.

FOR REFLECTION AND RESPONSE

Begin by journaling, using the following questions:

1. When have I experienced recurring sexual fantasies and images?

2. When have I pursued a pattern of sexual activity that might be considered addictive?

3. When and where did these thoughts, fantasies or practices begin?

There may have been a point when you chose to follow an addictive path or when someone close to you led you into sin. In that case it will be important to confess that early choice as the sin that it is, or to renounce that relationship as the negative influence it was.

4. With whom could I share these struggles? Often a part of deliverance involves confessing our sins to one another that we might be healed (see James 5:14-16).

5. With whom could I pray about these sensitive and vulnerable issues? Prayer with a person of the same sex is crucial at these sensitive points. You will want to pray with someone, or with a team of people, who has experienced this healing and deliverance themselves. If you will be praying for hatred-of-women issues, you will want the people you pray with to include a healthy woman who can lay hands on you. It is often unwise for men to lay hands on women who have experienced and internalized hatred of women. The response to men at the moment of healing can be a bit terrifying, as rage and fear come out and onto the cross of Jesus.

Here then are the prayers that I learned in the Pastoral Care Ministry conferences and that I have often used in group environments for deliverance from the gods of sexual obsession in our culture. These prayers are not to be used lightly. Pastoral insight, wisdom and spiritual authority are crucial. Once again, do not think of yourself more highly than you ought to think, but with sober judgment, each according to the measure of faith God has given you (Romans 12:3).

Invite the presence and power and protection of the Holy Spirit. *Come, Holy Spirit, now.*

Confess past choices, failures and sins. An addictive or demonic influence may well go back a generation or more in your family; if so, like Gideon in the Old Testament, you will need to renounce those family line sins.

We chose Baal. Our fathers chose Baal.

We have come to renounce the idol god of Baal in our lives, our families, our churches, our nation.

I renounce you, Baal, in the holy name of Jesus.

I renounce you, Ashtoreth, in the holy name of Jesus.

You may also have to renounce the devaluing and even hatred of women that sexual addiction often involves. If you are a man, you may need to renounce the sin of misogyny (hatred of women). If you are a woman, you may have internalized a sense of self-hatred.

I renounce the sin of the hatred of women. By your grace now the effects will leave my mind and body.

I renounce the idols my father served. I renounce the idols my mother served.

Next, when we have invited God's presence, we ask God to show us any demonic presence in our life, and we wait and listen to God's Spirit. Sometimes an image comes to mind. Sometimes images stream and even cascade through our mind. Or we may have a sense of a presence we were unaware of.

Now manifest, unclean and unholy spirit. Show me, Spirit of God, any demonic presence in my life and heart.

Then we pray for the cleansing consuming presence of God. We confess that we live under the authority of Jesus, that demons have no place in our life and no right to remain. If it is part of your practice to pray in tongues, now is a good time.

Come, holy fire of God, and strike any vile image. Cleanse me and fill me, Lord. I confess that Jesus is my Lord and that no other has any right to rule or influence me. Any other presence must leave now, in the name of Jesus.

Ask your friend, prayer partner or counselor to pray for your cleansing and filling. Explain any ways you feel stuck or need more from God's Spirit. Pray for the power of any sexual addiction to be broken in your life.

If appropriate, pray also for the power of the hatred of women to be broken in your life. Confess that sin, whether you are a man or a woman, and confess any ways that hatred of women has led you to hurt others or hate yourself. Pray for deliverance from evil!

Then praise God and ask for his filling in any place from which an alien presence has fled.

Praise you, Jesus. We give you thanks. Fill us with your Holy Spirit, as gentle as a dove. May this healing continue, Lord.

End with songs of praise that celebrate God's victory and God's holy presence with you! You may want to sing "Holy, Holy, Holy" or "A Mighty Fortress."

Remember always to stay focused on the presence of Christ and not on the demonic. And remember, whenever you renounce the influence of an evil spirit, you must ask to be filled with the Holy Spirit. Nature abhors a vacuum.

Isn't it good news for our hearts and for our world that Jesus has triumphed over the demonic through his death and resurrection, and that we can experience new dimensions of sexual freedom and purity? Amen. May God make it so!

Healing, Sacraments and Touch

Dan and Melissa approached MaryKay and me during the Communion service Sunday morning at our church. MaryKay and I had attended Church of the Resurrection, an Anglican church in the western suburbs of Chicago, for several years. The leaders of this church deeply understood the connection between the sacraments and healing. Every Sunday, after Communion, people were invited to receive prayer from prayer ministers standing in the side aisles. Dan and Melissa had been involved in Church of the Resurrection and were now leaving to carry the vision for healing to a church in Canada. Melissa later wrote:

> Our last prayer session rolled up together all we had learned and wanted to pass along. MaryKay prayed for Dan and blessed the healing he had received for his sense of being and well-being. Warmth went into his soul, and the peace of God suffused his being. He had taken Communion and felt strengthened by God, and now he felt the pleasure and nurture of God

filling him as he faced a new calling in a new location. Rick then put his hands on Dan's head and blessed him, confirming his calling to evangelism and to teaching, anointing his forehead with oil. Dan's lips burned, and his heart pounded.

Then Rick placed his hands on my hands, positioned above my heart. Rick blessed the healing of the father wound that I had experienced at a recent conference. I sensed the renewal and the strengthening of God's fatherly blessing upon me. God was using a man and a father as a channel to pour out God's fatherly blessing on me. I felt led to confess a fear of abandonment that I had dwelled on and obsessed about over the last days, and MaryKay pronounced me forgiven on the authority of Scripture. Then she washed my forehead with water as a symbol of the cleansing of my mind and thoughts. Then Rick and MaryKay hugged us and sent us off with love.

We left church that morning strengthened and encouraged, full of hope and vision, with a sense that God had called us to go and that God would provide and anoint us for ministry and service and leadership. In the months that followed, that precious time of prayer and commissioning remained a living memory that helped us through the hard times of transition. We are so thankful for a church that believes that God heals and that understood how God uses men and women, Communion and blessed water, touch and "words" to heal us and call us. Thank you!

This chapter will explore the physical and sacramental means God has given us for healing. The potency of these avenues for healing resides in the way God always comes to us in this world: through *incarnation*.

Melissa and Dan's prayer experience encapsulates a great deal of truth about how God works! God used the presence and touch of a

---

SIGNPOST 1
Learn to practice God's presence and to hear God's still small voice.

SIGNPOST 2
Replace diseased images and memories of God and human beings with healed and transformed images.

SIGNPOST 3
Renounce unreal identities. Discern and embrace your real identity.

SIGNPOST 4
Get at the roots of pain and problems, not just the fruits or symptoms.

SIGNPOST 5
Use the physical and sacramental means God has given as channels of healing power.

SIGNPOST 6
Turn outward! Healing that empowers compassion and service in the world is true healing.

---

woman and a man, a holy hug, oil of anointing, bread and wine, and spoken words of nurture and blessing to fill their souls and memories with his love, nurture and healing power.

Culturally we tend toward a disembodied, superspiritual understanding of how God heals and works. But God's pattern in the world is incarnation. He fills material things and human hands with his presence to heal and to save. Flesh and blood, bread and wine, oil and water are among the material things that God uses as bridges into our bodily reality.

That's the way God worked in Christ. He didn't come to us as pure spirit. God came to us as a flesh-and-blood Jew, a baby born in a shed, a carpenter's son. He walked among us, often tired and hungry, weeping and laughing, striding the earth as a man. He lived under oppression, felt the sting of poverty and the whip, endured rejection and humiliation. He can sympathize with us in our weakness because he is one of us and endured all the shame, humiliation, vulnerability and pain that we endure.

CELEBRATE THE INCARNATION!

If we follow Jesus, we all believe in the incarnation. But often we fail to grasp the implications of the incarnation for how God works in the world—the way God has *always* worked.

Many of us have essentially an ancient Greek view of matter and spirit: we think spirit is good and matter is bad. We are uncomfortable with our passions, our hunger for food, our love of sex, our enjoyment of pleasure. The ancient Greeks, especially the Stoics, believed that the way to become whole is to control and even repress the passions. Passion is the enemy of the good, some Greeks believed.

This view is pernicious and wholly un-Christian and unbiblical. God loves matter: he made it. God loves desires: he gave them to us. Satan has never created a new desire or a true need. He can only counterfeit and mutilate what God has designed and brought to life.

Our God is a God of passion. He is a suffering God. When some early Greeks got hold of the doctrine of God, they turned God into an unchangeable being "without passions or parts." It's just not true. Our God is a jealous God. Our God is vitally involved in his world. Our God is passionate. Our God suffered and died on a Roman cross.

Sometimes when we think of the death of Jesus—the doctrine of the atonement—we make a distinction between the Father and the Son, as if one part of God was angry at sin and poured out that anger on another part of God, who suffered, loved and died. That's a wrong way of thinking. The truth is all of God is angry at the destruction that sin has wrought, and all of God suffered at the cross. Father and

Son may have suffered in different ways and expressed hatred for sin in different ways. But Father and Son are one and participated fully together in all that happened.

God likes matter. God likes passion. God made us with needs and desires. God comes to us in very physical ways.

How you explain the relationship between spirit and matter will depend partly on your denominational tradition. For my part, I am most comfortable with the language of "real presence" when talking about Communion or baptism. God is really present in the elements of bread, wine, water, though not to make them magical and operative even when faith is absent. When God's people come together, God fills those elements with his grace and ministers healing and sustenance through them as people receive them in faith.

Seeing the sacraments as I do may not square with your theological tradition. But I want to challenge you to become more open to God's using human flesh and touch—laying on of hands, anointing with oil, washing with water, feeding with bread and wine (or grape juice!). The incarnation of Jesus, the Spirit filling human flesh, is the way God works in the world. That's why Paul laid hands on Timothy and others to stir up spiritual gifts and pass on spiritual authority. That's why in Acts 19 handkerchiefs healed people. That's why elders are to anoint the sick with oil.

God's presence often comes to us through physical and fleshy channels.

When I pray for healing, I am very aware of this dynamic. As I mentioned earlier, when I pray for being and well-being, I place one hand over a person's back and one over his heart (I have a woman cross her hands over her heart, and I place my hand over hers). I pray over the heart because I am praying for God's presence to enter into the person's body at the very point of need. The physical placement is a sign of the spiritual reality. A healthy woman has a special ability to be an incarnational channel of God's nurturing presence to the sufferer.

When I pray for cleansing, I often use water to symbolize it. As a priest, I bless that water using ancient prayers.[1] But if blessing water is uncomfortably foreign to you, don't do it. You can use water as a symbol for cleansing anyway. God can deeply minister to the sufferer who carries debilitating shame through the application of water that symbolizes God's cleansing.

When you pray for someone younger to be used of God, lay your hands on their head, shoulder or hands. Pray God's blessing and anointing. God can use the touch of an older man or woman powerfully, to bless and to fill that person with his Spirit.

When someone is sick, use oil to anoint them, and then pray. Oil is a sign of the Spirit in both the New Testament and the Old. And oil is a sign of reconciliation and the joy of reconciliation, as in Psalm 133.

When you celebrate Communion, learn from the liturgical traditions that know how to *celebrate*. Too many churches make Communion a very solemn, introspective, individualistic experience. More ancient traditions call Communion the Eucharist, the Great Thanksgiving. As we worship God in joy for Jesus' death and resurrection and receive the elements of bread and wine, our souls are strengthened. In many liturgical traditions the center and climax of the service is Communion, not the sermon. There is something powerful and healthy about proclaiming Jesus' death and resurrection every single week, not just in words but through the powerfully symbolic acts of setting apart simple bread and wine to be the body and blood of Jesus.

When you celebrate baptism, seek to recover a fuller understanding of its meaning. In the early church baptism was the most joyful and powerful service of the church year. Often baptisms happened at Easter, or during the Easter vigil the night before. The whole period of Lent, the six weeks preceding Good Friday and Easter, was seen as preparation. Often new converts focused on learning about the

Christian faith for the three years before they were baptized, and then they used Lent as a time of spiritual preparation and battle. They recognized not only their sin but their idolatry, their bent-over posture, their vulnerabilities to the work of Satan and the ways of the world.[2]

As noted earlier, candidates for baptism in the early church prayed to renounce Satan and his works, the world and its ways, and the flesh and its sins. Baptism wasn't just about forgiveness of sin; it was also about freedom from addiction and slavery and being bent toward competitors for the worship of God. People had a much fuller understanding of salvation and therefore experienced deeper healing at baptism. No wonder there was such a release of energy and joyful celebration in baptismal services. These great services of the church can be times of profound healing for God's people.

It is important to give a couple of cautions about touch. It is best always to *ask* people if it is okay to lay your hands on them while praying. If a person has had an abusive background, particularly if he or she has suffered sexual abuse—or even if they are just from a Northern European country, like Sweden!— your touch will be uncomfortable unless it has been invited. In addition, when you pray for a woman who has been affected by the hatred of women, it is important for women to extend touch as they are being healed. In such a situation male touch will often cause a very negative reaction. I found out about that the hard way once!

God works through flesh and blood, bread and wine, oil and water, touch and sign. God loves matter: it is his creation. God loves desires, blesses passions, comes to us in the humility of human form. Embrace and practice the many incarnational channels God has given us for healing. Whatever your background and denomination, make greater room for God to come physically, through human flesh and blood.

Let us celebrate the incarnation! God became human. God heals us through flesh-and-blood channels. That's the way God works.

16

The Healing Journey and the Outward Journey

Sam approached me for prayer during the Sunday morning service. My heart fell a bit. It seemed that Sam approached me for prayer at least once a month, and each time he told the same story, though the names had changed. He was depressed. He struggled with same-sex attraction. He had experienced another breakup with a girlfriend.

I had heard others' reports of these kinds of struggles and loved praying for them. But somehow praying for Sam drained me. I kept getting the sense that he was fascinated by his inner world, that he never could get enough of talking about himself and contemplating the ups and downs of his feelings and inner experiences.

Sam's mom had been very caring and his dad very distant. His mother had never disciplined him, and he was very oriented toward himself. So he struggled with distance from his dad and alienation from his own gender identity, but he also struggled with immense self-centeredness stemming from his mother's bentness toward him. She had raised a selfish son.

This Sunday morning, during Communion, I decided to try another track with Sam. I challenged him to stop looking for healing, to stop asking for healing prayer, to stop focusing on his inner woundedness. Enough already! Hasn't he gotten tired of himself? I asked him, "If you want prayer, what could we pray for together that involves other people and their needs and concerns?" Running through my mind were the words of C. S. Lewis, "Can you for one moment think about something not yourself?"

Needless to say, Sam stopped asking me for prayer!

Ministries of healing prayer attract broken, needy people who at some point may need to *stop* seeking their own healing and start focusing on others and engaging with the world around them. Some people like nothing better than to get lost in their inner world. Sadly,

SIGNPOST 1
Learn to practice God's presence and to hear God's still small voice.

SIGNPOST 2
Replace diseased images and memories of God and human beings with healed and transformed images.

SIGNPOST 3
Renounce unreal identities. Discern and embrace your real identity.

SIGNPOST 4
Get at the roots of pain and problems, not just the fruits or symptoms.

SIGNPOST 5
Use the physical and sacramental means God has given as channels of healing power.

SIGNPOST 6
Turn outward! Healing that empowers compassion and service in the world is true healing.

misguided prayer ministers often foster such a dramatically self-centered orientation.

The Christian journey involves giving away in love all that God has given us. We find our lives by losing them. And we are truly healed in our inward life as we grow in our capacity to both give and receive in healthy ways. Let's look at four stages in the outward journey that correspond with real steps toward maturity along the inward journey of healing.

PRAYING FOR OTHERS

As we begin to receive healing of our brokenness, we soon want to pray for others. As we have received, we want to give. And often we have the most to give in the particular ways God has been giving to us. One of the most delightful things to the heart of God, and one of the most upsetting things for Satan, is that God so often brings good out of what was meant for evil. We see God bringing good out of evil in Scripture accounts. For instance, God delighted to turn the murdering Pharisee Saul into the suffering apostle Paul. And we see this pattern of God's redemptive work today too. God loves to turn the anxious, empty woman into a wellspring of nurture and well-being for others. God loves to turn the insecure and self-conscious man into a deep source of masculine blessing to others. Our places of hurt, as we are healed, become sources of insight and healing for others.

We begin this dimension of the outward journey by asking God for opportunities to pray for others and taking those opportunities as they come.

You can start by gathering a group to study this book with a few others. Pray the prayers given here for one another. Make sure to seek out mentoring from others who have gone before you on the journey and can give you wise counsel.

Next begin to pray for the establishment of a prayer ministry in your church. In part one of appendix three, "The Leadership Journey in Healing Prayer," you'll find recommendations for how to go about beginning a prayer ministry in your church.

When you receive healing through prayer, there is a strong temptation to sit back and remain passive and receptive. Yet the irony is that often the deepest healing you will receive will come as you give to others what you have begun to receive.

Is there a danger here? Might you try to pray for others too early, before you have sufficient perspective on your own pain and God's work in your life? My sense is that God often wants us just to receive for a while, maybe a month, maybe up to six months, depending on the severity of the issues we need to walk through. But usually sooner rather than later, and often before you feel ready, God will want you to begin to pray for one or two others. If you don't make that turn outward, you will be in danger of getting stuck within your own feelings and experiences. Truly, the healing you hope for will quickly disappear if you remain focused inward for too long.

A good test: Ask those who have prayed for you if they think it is time for you to begin praying for others in the ways you have received prayer. Listen well to what they tell you. Then as you launch into ministry, pair up with someone who has been praying for others for a while. You are probably not ready to claim much authority or expertise, so you will want to take it slowly. But in order to truly become healed and not just have cool healing experiences, you need to give away what you are receiving.

PRAYING FOR SEEKING FRIENDS

A second dimension in the outward journey is a desire to pray with and for friends, family members and others who do not know God yet. God's presence has become more real to you, God's voice more cherished. You may find yourself with new love for people outside

God's family. The good news of the gospel has begun to get at your areas of brokenness. Maybe until now you weren't entirely convinced or passionate about God's reality and God's power. You have been a Christian, but the good news about Jesus hadn't been deeply good and transforming till recently. Now you're starting to sense a new passion to help others taste and see that the Lord is good.

In my experience, when we pray for physical healing for people already in God's family, God sometimes answers those prayers. But I have more often seen God work powerfully as I pray for physical healing for my seeking friends.

My friend Sam works at Einstein Bagel's, where I write my books. I have often prayed for him to find his wallet or for God to heal his ulcer problems. And God seems to love answering those prayers for Sam more than answering similar prayers for me!

Here's how I understand this: God wants to make his rule and authority especially tangible for people who are not following him. So sometimes God answers my simple prayers for Sam. I think God has a different priority for me. God wants a deeper maturity from me, a love that is not dependent on God's finding me parking places or healing my sniffles or even more serious illnesses.

How do we pray for people who are not yet Christ followers? We listen as they express needs and offer to pray for them when they do. Many times I have told Sam that I am praying for some need of his. It has almost become our little joke. He always tells me, "It can't hurt." And he is beginning to believe that it really helps. Our culture affirms loving others and being spiritual, so an offer to pray is often welcomed.

When is it appropriate to pray with a seeking friend in their presence? Whenever I have a conversation of some depth with someone who isn't a Christ follower, if he has been honest about his needs, and if we are in a place where I can pray for him without drawing attention, I will ask if I can do that.

Once while riding a train in Amsterdam, I got into a conversation with a man who had many years before considered himself a Christian but had made choices that cut him off from his roots. He had recently visited the red-light district where prostitutes ply their trade. He was seeking comfort for his aching loneliness and the misery of his self-centeredness. When we got off the train on a side street, I offered to pray for him. Enough trust had been built through our conversation for him to want that. I prayed for God's blessing and healing. I asked God to minister to the lonely space within him, which he had sought to fill by seeking comfort with prostitutes, resulting in even deeper loneliness. I prayed about his broken relationship with a woman and his hurt, anger and even bitterness over it. I prayed for God's presence to nudge him to turn around and go back toward God, and to seek and find forgiveness for his choices.

At the end he looked at me with great longing in his eyes, saying he had felt the presence of God and a sense of peace that he had not experienced for years. He seemed to want to stand on the street corner and keep soaking it in. As we parted, he asked me to keep praying for him.

The power of healing prayer for seeking and skeptical people is recognized in the design of the Alpha curriculum. Alpha is a ten-week course for seekers and skeptics on the basics of the Christian faith. In the middle of the ten-week course there is a weekend retreat. Saturday night, after teaching for the day about the Holy Spirit, we invite the Spirit to minister healing and give gifts.

Often the only real barrier to praying healing for seekers is our lack of bold faith to believe God for a tangible expression of God's presence and power. Yet praying in the Spirit for seekers and skeptics is very exciting. God loves to bless this kind of prayer. I have found that God can't wait to "show up" for people who are not yet followers of Christ but are genuinely seeking. I have also noticed that once seeking or skeptical people commit themselves to Christ, they often do not have nearly as many barriers to believing that God can heal as many long-time Christians do. If you long to see God work in prayer and healing in the lives of your seeking or skeptical friends and family members, you can get more help in my book *Evangelism Outside the Box*.[1]

Few activities head off the dangers and dead ends of prayer ministry like turning outward and praying for healing for spiritual seekers and skeptics. May God empower you to take risks and trust God to work!

INTEGRATION

Integration, a third stage in the outward journey, is a movement that corresponds to increasing maturity in the journey of healing. In this stage, healing prayer becomes less of a stand-alone practice and starts being integrated into a larger life of practicing God's presence for service in the world. We think less about our own anxiety, trauma and past hurts and more about the inward and outward disciplines that help us feed on Christ and serve others. Fasting and prayer, study and worship, sabbath and solitude are crucial means for our inner person to be strengthened by the presence of God. As we are strengthened, we pursue service and celebration, witness and justice. Our lives are no longer so defined by what we have suffered. We cease to focus so much on our past as sexual addict, alcoholic, homosexual, depressive or dependent. These struggles may well continue, and sometimes in moments of stress we will feel as if we have made no progress at all. We may still need to reject destructive ways of comforting ourselves. But the focus of our life, the emphasis of our inner thoughts and outer actions, has shifted. It is no longer all about us. It never really was anyway.

It has been fascinating for me to watch this journey toward integration. Healing is still an important part of our story but no longer the key to the whole. Many people seek a spiritual director or mentor at this stage, and focus more on the spiritual disciplines than on spiritual healing. There is often a maturing shift from the question "How do I escape my pain?" toward the question "What is God saying in the midst of, and even through, my pain?"

HEALING SOCIETIES AND NATIONS

A fourth dimension of the outward journey corresponding to increasing maturity is pursuit of reconciliation ministry. Healing prayer is no longer motivated by a desire to ease our pain, nor even to achieve individual wholeness. Prayer ministry starts to become part of the larger work of God to reconcile divided peoples. It becomes a crucial way to extend God's rule over sundered human relationships.

The division may be between groups or churches. Churches often split; new denominations go their separate ways. Healing prayer can be instrumental in the reconciliation of churches and leaders alienated from one another. Several years ago I led a citywide concert of prayer at a large church in downtown Chicago. We spent time confessing our sins of mistrust and even hatred toward others of different denominations and churches. We even brought before God our memories of past church and denominational splits. That evening the pastor of a large evangelical church was reconciled to the pastor of a large Pentecostal church; twenty years earlier the latter congregation had split off from the former over the issue of charismatic gifts. This reconciliation was the high point of the evening for many of us, and a beginning of new relationships and partnerships for the gospel in Chicagoland.

I hope you are beginning to catch a vision and passion for this fourth stage of the outward journey. This stage involves applying the insights we gain in the healing journey to the bigger issues that face and sometimes tear apart the body of Christ.

Our world is a divided world. We are torn apart especially along racial and ethnic lines. The healing journey, as we begin to apply it to the broader ministry of reconciliation, has immense redemptive potential.

A few years ago three thousand people, mostly college students, gathered in a large assembly hall at the University of Illinois-Urbana for a prayer ministry session focused on ethnic and racial healing and reconciliation. African American pastor Brenda Salter McNeil and I taught about God's power to heal divisions between nations, peoples and ethnic groups. We spoke of the power of admitting our sins and even hatred of one another. We spoke of the power of God to take our rage, shame and guilt onto himself on the cross of Christ. We held up God's power to lift off shame and rage, to forgive sin and to heal our lands. I recounted the process of coming to grips with my own prejudices and racism as a white man.

Then we led the crowd in prayer. Many cried out to God. Many confessed their sins. Many looked to God for healing of their own ethnic identity and for the capacity to empathize with and love people who are different.

After a powerful time of healing, we invited forward those who wished to receive prayer individually. It was a profound picture of God's kingdom: people of every racial and ethnic background coming together, praying together and crying together. We issued a final challenge to the students to become God's reconciliation generation. The chord struck by this call and commission to this group was evident on nearly every upturned face. (You can read about our model of healing prayer for divided groups in appendix two.)

God is at work in a divided world to bring healing and reconciliation. We have barely begun to tap the power of the cross and the potency of God's presence to bring people together. I am convinced that the next mighty outpouring of God's Spirit will be marked by a focus on God's power to heal and reconcile divided races and ethnic groups. The promise of Jesus, that through our unity the world will know that the Father sent the Son, remains true and awaits an even broader demonstration in the years ahead.

Many church people misunderstand the reconciling work of God and criticize those of us who pursue it. Bridge people often experience redemptive suffering, based not so much on their own hurts and wounds as on identifying with Jesus' ministry to a broken world and church. Bridge people are often lonely, neither fully rooted in their own community nor fully accepted in the community toward which they build bridges.

Jesus was a bridge person in the ultimate sense, between heaven and earth, God and humanity. He has reconciled the world to himself through the cross and is looking forward to the day when all things in heaven and earth will be fully reconciled to God and to one another (see Colossians 1:15-20). He calls us into his ministry of reconciliation.

May God give us grace to pursue and apply the insights of the healing journey to a world that desperately needs mending and remaking.

And may God give us grace to let him turn our hurts into healing for others as we continue in the healing journey. May we undertake the outward journey of service and love as energetically as we pursue the inward journey toward wholeness. In the end they are the same journey.

FOR REFLECTION AND RESPONSE

1. Rick shares four stages in the outward journey. Where to you see yourself? How have you begun to give away what God has given you in healing?

2. Where would you most like to grow in the outward journey? What could help you grow?

17

Dangers and Dead Ends on the Healing Journey

Before we end our conversation, I need to speak of one more set of concerns. You will not find them in the signposts with which we started. But the issues in this chapter are so fundamental that they will affect whether you survive and thrive as you pursue the healing journey or whether your interest in and experience of healing dwindle over time.

At one point I needed a lot of healing for myself after being involved in a ministry of healing. As I watched what happened in that ministry, I began to recognize characteristic temptations that people who experience healing can fall into. I have come to understand some of the dangers in the ministry of healing, the potholes in the road, and the turns we can take that will lead us into dead ends and danger. These dangers and dead ends can all too quickly undermine and undo our own healing journey. It is crucial for us to reflect on these dangers so that we can avoid them and carry on in the journey of healing all the way to the end.

Many who read this book and experience healing will feel God's nudge to enter into a journey of leadership. You will want to pray for others and even teach and lead others into prayer ministry. You in particular need to read this chapter and be vigilant about these dangers.

Spiritual Pride and Elitism

The first temptation as we receive and minister healing prayer is the temptation toward pride and elitism. This is probably the most common and most deadly killer of healing prayer in the church. It can take several forms.

Often as we receive and minister in healing and transforming ways, we have an experience that can feel as dramatic as conversion. Immediately we think everyone needs to be doing what we are doing and experiencing what we have experienced. We can become very "evangelistic" about our experience. We can't imagine how other Christians could live without seeing what we have seen and experiencing God's work as we have.

When we received prayer, someone listened to God on our behalf and heard God speak in a way that overwhelmed us. *How could that person know I was feeling that way? How could they know about that event in my past? How could they speak just the words I needed to hear?* These experiences can be very powerful and leave their marks on us for life.

But it is crucial for us to receive such words and experiences with humility and wisdom. Nothing has hurt the expansion of the Holy Spirit's work as much as people's belief that they have reached a new level of spiritual insight and maturity just because they had a new experience—and their subsequent eager attempts to force the same experience on others. The test of any experience is the fruit it bears, and the primary fruit is our character. Our ability to love others, serve others and receive God's ministry with humility is the true test of the depth and substance of God's work in us. Spiritual pride and elitism are antithetical to the fruit of godly character, which God values above all else.

I have also noticed that prayer ministry tends to attract certain kinds of people. Of course deeply needy people are attracted, because they know their need for healing. But deeply needy people can then build their identity and sense of worth, and even superiority, around their new experience.

The other group of people often attracted to leadership in the ministry of healing consists of leaders who are intuitively or artistically gifted and have a strong need to feel special. What is more special than hearing from God? What is more awesome than a leader who sees into people's hearts and ministers transforming healing to the soul or body? But often these leaders have deep holes in their own heart. Maybe they didn't feel special when they were young. Maybe Mom wasn't able to give the attention or nurture that an infant needs to know he's special. When leaders who need to feel special engage in the ministry of healing, they can unconsciously put themselves at the center and draw people into what can only be called worship of the prayer minister.

Pride and elitism are deadly to the soul of the healing prayer minister and deadly to the maturing and healing of the souls of sufferers. This tendency goes a long way toward explaining why many healing ministries provide a great breakthrough for people initially but fail of their promise over the long run, sometimes leaving shattered people more in need of healing than ever.

For a fascinating story that explores the rise and fall of just such a prayer ministry leader, read Susan Howatch's novel *Glamorous Powers*.[1] Darrow, the protagonist, begins a healing prayer ministry that at first is very successful. Many people attend the services and find help. But as numbers grow, Darrow pressures himself more and more to perform. He *has* to see people healed. He has to succeed, or the ministry will fail and people will know he's a fraud. At the heart of his vulnerability to temptation is his need to feel special and to elicit others' worship.

People who care about Darrow begin to question and then confront him. They see his neediness and the drivenness of his efforts. But Darrow ignores the warning signs in himself and from others. He is unwilling to receive correction and be accountable, and so he becomes increasingly driven and isolated.

At one of his services he finally has a nervous breakdown while trying to bring healing to a particularly needy and ill group of people. The breakdown begins his very difficult journey back to health. He has to face what made him sick even as he tried to bring healing to others, and he has to face his self-isolation. The warning signs were there. Friends tried to bring accountability. But he went over the cliff of his weakness, his need to feel special.

Darrow's escalating disintegration is a powerful warning to all of us who have some of these gifts and vulnerabilities. Darrow's shadow side, that unconscious part of him that is driven, needy and self-deceiving, takes over his whole life and ministry. He seeks out and listens to no one who could confront and challenge him at the point of his destructive needs and drives.

Without interpersonal accountability, community and even confrontation at points, any of us will live blissfully at first and later miserably, unaware of our shadow side until it leads us into a crisis, even into disintegration.

Another temptation toward spiritual pride lies in the tendency to pray in ways that express great authority, even grandiosity. Sometimes people speak in prayer to Satan and demons, casting them out of persons and even whole cities or nations. The practice of rebuking Satan and casting ruling demons out of cities is misguided at best and often very dangerous. All we do is call attention to ourselves. As the seven sons of Sceva learned (Acts 19), being presumptuous and over-reaching our authority out of a drive for spiritual power and grandiosity can get us beat up badly.

In general, let Jesus and his angels fight the battles over cities, as illustrated in Daniel 10:12-14, where angels are reported to have battled a spiritual being called the prince of Persia. If you encounter demons in people, deal with them. Better yet, if you are praying for a committed Christian, have that person renounce them and take his or her place in Christ. But don't seek them out or take them on unnecessarily.

I am not saying that no one should pray in larger, grander ways. Maybe God specifically calls some people to do that. I don't want to set myself up as their judge. But most of us will do well to live our little lives trusting our big God to take on "higher-level" spiritual warfare, for which there is not much scriptural support anyway, at least in terms of the actual practice.

DEPENDENCY ON HEALING EXPERIENCES OR PRAYER MINISTERS

In addition to the dangers of pride and elitism, issues of dependency can pose serious dangers. We can be tempted to become dependent on the healing experience and keep seeking to have it over and over, like a three-year-old who keeps repeating, "Again . . . Again . . . Do it again." Healing experiences are intended to lead us toward maturity, not dependency on a person or experience.

In our culture we have a strong experience orientation that can keep us seeking a repeat of adrenaline-inducing events. Again, this search is a sign of immaturity and not growth.

We can also become dependent on a certain prayer minister and feed off his or her energy rather than looking to Christ. Or if we are a prayer minister, we may engender others' dependency. The unique intimacy that comes with praying for others' healing holds great power, and we must manage that power wisely.

After one teaching session on healing, my co-teacher and I met for prayer with a man struggling with homosexuality. As he shared his struggles honestly, we began to pray. We sensed family background issues and prayed for those. We grieved his losses. We prayed prayers of confession for his sinful choices. At one point I stood back and realized we were doing all the work. My prayer colleague and I were grieving, repenting, praying, renouncing. And this struggler was lapping it all up, basking in the attention, feeding off our energy. We were all reinforcing one another's sickness, not helping one another toward health. At that moment I asked him if he wanted healing and repentance. He wasn't sure that he did, so our prayer session ended right then.

THE NEED TO BE NEEDED

You may be a person who needs to be needed. Such people are often drawn into the ministry of prayer. In our culture women have been encouraged to find affirmation and even personal identity by meeting the needs of others. But there is a difference between serving people and trying to save them. It is a fine line. Your shadow side, unknown to you, may be driving you to meet your own deep needs by engendering others' dependency. Yet you may also be very afraid of others' depending on you. You feel needy inside, afraid of being used up emotionally. So one moment you invite people in and the next moment you are running away.

These tendencies must be named and faced, and that can happen only as you share your soul with peers and mentors. Again, community and wise accountability are crucial to maintaining the health of healing ministries and of prayer ministers over the long haul.

I had to face my own temptation toward engendering dependency on me among those I prayed for. The intimacy of prayer ministry was very nurturing, for the person I prayed for but also for me. When I prayed for others I was able to feel nurtured and yet remain in a position of power over them. In that way I got the nurture I needed without risking my own heart.

This temptation is especially common when men pray for women. Sadly, many affairs have begun apparently very innocently as people prayed for one another. Pastors are very susceptible to this way of meeting their own needs.

It may be surprising, but many pastors, prayer ministers and counselors go into the people-helping business in part because of our own need for healing, love and affirmation. For Christian leaders and prayer ministers, it is crucial to get in touch with our neediness, embrace it and live humbly in its light. We are very dangerous to ourselves and to others when we haven't faced our shadow side. And we are very dangerous when we are not in community and accountability with others regarding our temptations and neediness. It is very important that counselors have their own counselor to keep them accountable and self-aware.

But pastors and prayer ministers often have no community or supervision to address their temptations and weaknesses. One of the great barriers to overcome is the shame we feel about our vulnerabilities. Listen, you probably wouldn't be helping others, counseling others, nurturing others or praying for others if you didn't have profound needs yourself. Can't we just admit that? Can't we all seek the help we need?

I just prayed with a pastor and prayer leader. He has struggled for twenty-five years with what he considers a particularly embarrassing temptation. He had never before told anyone about it. He cried out, "How can I be a pastor and prayer leader and also have this struggle?" Well, I had news for him. He probably would never have become a pastor and prayer leader if he hadn't had such brokenness in his life. And he certainly wouldn't have been as sensitive, humble and effective as he is without that experience of brokenness and sin. God loves to redeem us and use us at the point of our greatest weakness. But we have to get over the shame, come into the light and be willing to seek out the accountability and help we need.

If you are a leader who does prayer ministry, I want to ask you: Whom do you share your soul with? Who helps you with your temptations and vulnerabilities? Who keeps you accountable? If you have no one, then maybe you should step back from active ministry and leadership until you do. This appeal is not just to those who are starting out. It is *especially* directed to those who have been in ministry and leadership for years. If you don't have intimate, genuine honesty and accountability with someone else, someone who is in a position to challenge you without losing their job, their standing, their ministry or their relationship with you, your shadow side may well be causing more damage than you can possibly realize. Or it soon may.

THE SHADOW SIDE OF EMPATHY

I want to discuss one more dimension of the temptation toward dependency. I call this dimension the tendency to overempathize.

Ann was a partner on a team I led that traveled to college campuses to share the gospel. In addition to training students in evangelism, our team prayed for people. We prayed for Christian students, many of whom were beleaguered and hurting. We also prayed for student seekers and skeptics, believing that God can touch people and persuade them more compellingly with his presence than with any argument we could make.

After one visit Ann was depressed. She couldn't figure out why. The visit had gone very well, but she couldn't shake the depression. As we prayed we discovered a couple of things. First, Ann had been very affected by the spiritual environment of the campus. Second, she had prayed with someone suffering from depression. What she was feeling now wasn't actually her depression. By overly identifying with the sufferer for whom she prayed, she had taken into herself the other person's depression! When she renounced that person's depression and remembered that she was herself and not the other person, the depression lifted immediately.

Overidentification, exaggerated empathy, is very common in prayer ministry. In extreme forms it can lead to the practice of substitution, in which the prayer minister asks to take on some of the sufferer's pain, so that the sufferer's burden is relieved. Even as great a soul as C. S. Lewis attempted such substitution when his wife struggled with painful cancer.

The problem with substitution is pride, even though we are often hooked first by compassion. Jesus alone is the sin bearer. He bears our wounds as well. We ask him to take sin and suffering into himself. That is not our role. We are not the Messiah. We are his servants. We are ministering servants and not the suffering sacrifice.

I once was part of a prayer session in which a minister asked that a disease be lifted off a sufferer and distributed among each of us who were praying. Without hesitating a second, I renounced that prayer! Then I asked Jesus to take the sin and suffering onto himself at the cross and to heal the body and soul of the sufferer. I know it probably embarrassed the person who had prayed, but these prayers are just too real and potent to be played with.

PROMISING OR SEEKING THE QUICK FIX

Along with the tendency toward dependency on the prayer minister or prayer experience, we who give and receive prayer can also be tempted to promise or seek quick fixes. Wouldn't it be wonderful if God would just intervene, heal us and remove all the pain in our heart and body?

People often seek prayer not really to get better but to *feel* better. If the pain can be lessened or removed, our goal in seeking prayer will be realized. Here's one of the problems with that goal: in any process of healing, things often get worse before they get better. Our addictive practices, the ways we seek to comfort ourselves and assuage our pain, often work in the short run. We feel better for the moment. Of course we live in an inescapable vicious cycle that will never lead to healthy relationships and patterns of behavior. But just to feel better for a moment can seem worth all the future pain and shame and stuckness.

Mario Bergner calls the initial phase of moving toward healing "redemptive suffering," when we say no to the things and repetitive activities that bring comfort and a momentary escape from pain.[2] After he committed himself to coming out of homosexuality, he had to lock himself in his apartment for a whole weekend, two agonizing days and nights that seemed to stretch on forever. Denied the release of homosexual activity, he felt even more deeply his pain, loneliness, emptiness. But he knew that if he caved at this point, it might damage his chances for healing irreparably. He made it through that weekend and on into the rest of his healing journey. But his current leadership and joy in living had to come through the dark valley of that desolate weekend, without the sexual experience of comfort and release he had turned to many times before.

Until we have renounced all our destructive ways of seeking comfort and escape and are willing and able to face our inner pain, we will not make much progress in healing and sanctification. Of course in order to face the pain and turn away from addictive forms of comfort, we will need support, and a lot of it. We may need to lock ourselves in our apartment for a weekend, as Mario did. But mostly we need people around us who care for us, with whom we can be honest, who can keep speaking truth in love to us, being present emotionally and often physically.

Sometimes God heals us of some habit or addiction instantly. But mostly healing is a long obedience in the direction of conformity to Christ. Looking at Jesus, we are healed step by step, being transformed one day at a time. Healing is for getting better and not just for feeling better.

THE NEED TO PERFORM

One of the causes of promising the "quick fix" is our need to perform.

Have you ever looked into the eyes of a suffering person and wanted to see them get relief immediately? Have you ever prayed for someone, knowing that it was a big step for her to ask and that she asked because she thought you could really help? Have you ever promised people that God wants to help and to heal, and then had someone come to you for prayer, wanting to believe it's true but afraid it couldn't be true for her?

If you've ever faced any of these situations, then you know the pressure to perform that you can feel at such moments. The sufferer is crying out for help and healing, and you are crying out for God to give you some word, some insight, some way to pray that will help.

I find this pressure to perform and fear of failing at prayer ministry holds many of us back both from offering to pray and from asking for prayer. Then when we do pray, we can become self-consciously anxious about whether we are helping or not, whether God can use us this way or not.

In many cases the pressure to perform has led to truly horrendous coping mechanisms. Faith healers claim that God wants to heal and that if you have sufficient faith you will be healed. When you are not, it is because you didn't have faith. You were already hurting; on top of your initial pain, you are told that you don't even have faith the size of a mustard seed. Otherwise you would be healed. Now you are both sick and inadequate.

At some point all of us feel the pressure to perform. What is the antidote? Confess the self-consciousness, give the results to God, and focus on loving the person well. If you love the person well, that alone will bring good fruit. And if you can love well and forget for a moment about your own performance, God will have much more space to whisper wisdom to your soul for them.

OVERSPIRITUALIZING

Another common danger in ministries of healing is a tendency to overspiritualize reality, especially human psychology. Ancient worldviews superspiritualized from the ground up. Ancients saw spiritual causes behind every event. Spiritual beings ran the world, and misfortune was caused by the anger of the gods. The world was a place of mystery and misery, inhabited by unseen beings and powers who were constantly manipulating events and people's lives—often in chaotic ways.

People saw sickness, physical or psychological, as a result of the action of invisible spiritual beings and forces. Thus the doctors' role was primarily spiritual. Shamans and medicine men and women restored the balance of the forces and appeased angry spirits and gods. Since the causes of sickness were primarily spiritual, the cure was primarily spiritual.

There are many people today who embrace the ancient worldview. They reject modern medicine and put all their trust in faith healing and spiritual remedies. These people can be very dangerous and destructive to themselves and others. Newspapers carry stories of people who wouldn't take medicine or allow their children to get an injection that might have saved their life. Practices like snake handling are rooted in this worldview.

Some extreme healing ministries, whose leaders embrace a spiritualized view of reality, practice deliverance as the primary or only method of healing. They see every problem as demonic and cast out demons as the universal cure. There are demons of backaches, demons of colds, demons of depression and demons of suicide. People are "cleansed" of these demons but then often need repeat or remedial treatments. People who look at life this way have remained in an ancient worldview in which the spiritual explains everything that happens.

But spiritualizing every problem is not a danger only for extreme healing ministries. Almost always ministries of healing and people drawn to them fall into some degree of superspirituality, claiming instantaneous healing when it hasn't happened and spiritualizing important dimensions of human psychology.

Christian faith is incarnational. Body and spirit, emotions and will, angels and demons, the divine and the human are all inextricably interconnected, one great tapestry called reality. Since the incarnation in Jesus, when God became flesh and the Spirit came to us in human form, it can be no other way. Pull on any one thread and eventually the whole tapestry will unravel. There is no way to segment and box up the various dimensions of reality.

An incarnational worldview embraces the insights of ancient religions about the necessity of spiritual harmony and the impact of spiritual conflict. But the incarnational worldview also embraces the insights of medicine, physics, chemistry and math. The Christian worldview does not fragment reality but unifies it. Thus we can seek medical cures and spiritual cures, knowing that they work together and need each other.

There are many subtle ways that an overspiritualizing tendency shows up in healing ministries and practices. Often underlying the search for the quick fix is a superspiritual worldview. Many people believe God reaches down into our reality and fixes things and people if we just have faith. They may claim that healing should always be instantaneous and complete. The assumption that if you weren't healed, you lacked faith not only puts on performance pressure but betrays a superspiritual worldview.

Even the statement "God is in control" can become a trite cliché if by it we mean God is manipulating every little thing that happens. Again we have departed from an incarnational and biblical understanding of God as working through and collaborating with the flesh-and-blood beings he has created, in the context and flow of history. And of course, in the superspiritual view of reality the problem of evil is insoluble. If God is directly willing and bringing about *everything* from some place outside it all, then God is too horrible to be believed in or trusted. He becomes the source of much that is evil.

Leaders of healing ministries must be ever vigilant to the tendency to overspiritualize the world and human psychology. The need for balance and maturity is immense. None of us will get it right, but it is crucial to try, with the humble awareness that we will have blind spots and self-deceptions along the way. Once again, this is a reason that all of us need relationships with people outside of our ministries to keep bringing perspective and accountability.

So use counseling and prayer together. Assume that problems are multidimensional, though we often must deal with just one dimension at a time. Don't fragment reality. Expect God to work mostly through a gradual process of transformation into likeness to Christ. Realize that you will have blind spots and need outside perspective.

MISUSING POWER

One great need in prayer ministry today is for us to develop an ethic for the use of this form of power. Psychotherapists' associations have spent immense amounts of time identifying and setting up protections against ways that the power they have over their clients can be misused and abused. In contrast, prayer ministers have spent very little time in profound reflection on the dangers of misuse and abuse of their great power over the souls of the people they help. The abuses have led to a general discrediting of prayer ministry among large numbers of believers. It is crucial for both those ministering healing and those receiving it to explore issues of ethics regarding the use of power in the ministry of prayer.

Because prayer ministry can touch people at the deepest places of their being, the person who helps others in prayer faces some unique temptations. Some of those are similar to the temptations counselors face. But there is also the dimension of spiritual power and the temptations associated with it. If we fail to address this, many people who have suffered spiritual abuse will remain resolutely closed to God's healing touch.

Further, I believe people who are strong in this kind of gifting are often prone to certain kinds of woundedness. We must become self-aware for our own health and character and for a healthy long-term impact on the people we serve.

The need for healthy self-awareness and supervision is acute in the dynamic that counselors call *transference*. Transference occurs when a client starts to see a counselor as a father or mother figure (or some other authority figure from their past) and "transfers" feelings from past experiences onto the counselor. The counselor becomes the father who abandoned or the mother who was controlling. Transference can be very helpful in the counseling process, as long as the counselor understands it and doesn't get hooked. When the counselor gets hooked and starts transferring onto the client feelings from past experiences—anger or frustration or feelings of failure—the relationship can get very messy. So counselors have supervisors with whom they can sort things out whenever they start to feel hooked.

Churches are filled with these same dynamics but rarely have any resources for dealing with them. The pastor or prayer minister becomes a father or mother figure for someone seeking help. At first the minister may be idealized, almost worshiped. The leader is the benevolent father or loving mother who was never there before.

When you are receiving such adoration and affirmation, don't be fooled. Sooner or later the other shoe will drop. You, the pastor or prayer leader, will do something to disappoint. Then anger, disappointment and even hatred will pour forth unexpectedly and intensely. Gossip and slander may begin to mount, and a church that had a very good ministry will lose morale, focus and vision.

At that point the pastor or leader can get quite discouraged and do something that really merits anger, like have an affair, or blow up at the congregation, or plunge into some addictive comforting behavior. Now the pastor or leader has been hooked and is transferring back onto congregation members or sufferers past experiences of hurt, rejection or failure. Counselors call the tendency to be hooked and transfer feelings and hurts back toward the counselee *counter-transference.*

In the church we don't understand transference, and neither do we understand countertransference, when the pastor or prayer leader gets hooked and responds in destructive ways. We desperately need wisdom, teaching, accountability and supervision to address these issues of the dynamics and uses of power in prayer ministry.

If you are on the leadership journey in healing prayer, I appeal to you: seek out a mentor or a peer group with whom to talk and pray through issues of power, transference and countertransference. As soon as you are feeling hooked or experiencing transference positively or negatively, find someone to talk it over with! An ethic for prayer ministry is proposed in part three of appendix three in this book.

FINAL CHALLENGE

For many years I met with two other men for prayer. We spent twenty-four hours together three times a year. These men were not involved in prayer ministry and had nothing to lose by confronting me. They accepted my gifts but were also deeply in touch with my weaknesses and areas of neediness. I brought personal nudges from God to them, and I shared experiences and struggles in prayer ministry with them. We had spent years together, so our community and accountability were genuine, not superficial or counterfeit. These men have regularly spoken truth into my life and given wisdom, perspective and challenge when I most needed them. Who knows where I would be without such loving and challenging friends.

The call to community, discernment and accountability is the theme of this chapter on dangers and dead ends on the healing journey. May God give us each grace to embrace our need for others, to seek them out, and to minister and receive with restraint, care and humility. And may God give us the guts to walk in a piercing honesty about our neediness, temptations and vulnerability.

We need not let the dangers and dead ends paralyze us. God deeply longs for us to walk the healing path, for ourselves and with others. As we ask God for help and for discerning mentors and friends, we will find that God cares much more about this ministry than we do. And God cares about those of us who minister as much as he cares about our ministries. God will keep us! God will provide!

FOR REFLECTION AND RESPONSE

1. To which dangers do you feel most vulnerable? Why do you think you might be vulnerable in these ways?

2. Where in your life do you experience community and accountability?

On a scale of 1 to 10, with 1 being "not at all" and 10 being "strongly," how much do you experience genuine community and accountability, where others know your strengths but also your weaknesses and areas of neediness, where they feel free to be honest and direct with you?

3. Is God nudging you to commit to regular prayer and accountability with a few friends? With whom, and how could you take the next steps?

Conclusion

Our journey together is almost done. But your journey toward healing may have just begun.

As you walk toward wholeness in Christ, be encouraged. Remember how far you have come. Even in our short time together, look at all the progress we have made. Remember our signposts:

SIGNPOST 1
Learn to practice God's presence and to hear God's still small voice.

SIGNPOST 2
Replace diseased images and memories of God and human beings with healed and transformed images.

SIGNPOST 3
Renounce unreal identities. Discern and embrace your real identity.

SIGNPOST 4
Get at the roots of pain and problems, not just the fruits or symptoms.

SIGNPOST 5
Use the physical and sacramental means God has given as channels of healing power.

SIGNPOST 6
Turn outward! Healing that empowers compassion and service in the world is true healing.

If God has been at work in you over our time together, think back on all he has taught you and *celebrate*! And begin to think about how God might want you to give to others what you have received.

Have you grown at all in your capacity to know God? Have the eyes of your heart been opened even a little?

Have your imaginative and intuitive capacities been healed or strengthened?

Have you heard any part of your true name? Have you lived any more fully into your true identity?

Have you renounced any bent-over postures toward other persons, things or experiences? Have you straightened up at all to look to Jesus?

Do you understand any better the roots of your struggles? Has God brought any healing in your primary relationships with parents or those who stood in their place?

Have any painful memories been ministered to by Jesus? Have you extended or received forgiveness from the heart?

Have you given to any other what you have begun to receive? Have you prayed for a friend, Christian or seeking, or for reconciliation with a person of another denomination, race or ethnicity?

If you have taken any steps or experienced any healing, give thanks! *Celebrate!* Journal about the ways God has worked. Hold on to his healing words and nurturing presence. Remember.

If you have a particularly encouraging work of God's healing in you or through you, feel free to let me know. I would love to celebrate with you! And maybe your story will help others. You can e-mail me at Rick_Richardson@ivstaff.org.

There is so much at stake in the healing journey. Your own transformation rides on it. And the transformation of a hate-filled, divided, chaotic world may ride on it as well. May God give us grace to pursue with all of our strength the healing journey that stretches on before us.

Appendix 1

On Biblical and Cultural Sources of the Self

How do we get and grow a real self? How do we even understand what the self is?

These questions have engaged philosophers, sociologists and theologians through the centuries. In every age, people have had differing understandings of the self, both from cultural perspectives and from biblical perspectives. I want to suggest that our vision and understanding of the self is based on the integration of cultural and biblical perspectives on the self. If we adopt a culture-bound vision of the self, we can fall into the temptation of using biblical means (for instance the ministry of healing prayer) to gain narcissistic ends. Understanding the ways the self has been viewed in various cultures can give us clues about the ways we can substitute a cultural view for a biblical and Christ-oriented view. But cultural views of the self, as they resonate with scriptural perspectives, also help us grasp how we gain and grow a real self and what it means for us to be created in the image of God. Philosophy and theology must be integrated in order to understand the self in relevant and concrete ways.

So let's look at cultural understandings of the sources and shape of the self through history and then apply a biblical critique.

THE POTENTIAL SELF

The ancient Greeks understood the self as *potential;* for them the destination or goal of life was to develop the self toward excellence. In classical culture the true self was equated with the potential self. The goal was the fulfillment of potential, along the lines of the development of one's highest powers. "Be all that you can be!" captures the Greek view of the self.

A biblical dimension of the self is certainly reflected here. We were created in the image of God with great potential. The destination of wholeness in Christ includes the fulfillment of our potential.

There is also a grave potential for idolatry, however, in the Greek view of the self. The statement that best captures this tendency is from the philosopher Protagoras: "Man is the measure of all things." When we define excellence only according to our own sense of our capacities and potential, we have set human beings in the place of God. An idolatry of human achievement is a danger for any ministry that pursues excellence and presupposes human capacity and goodness.

As I was growing up I loved the show *Star Trek.* Captain Kirk in the original series captures the humanistic view of the power of the can-do spirit to overcome any obstacle and conquer the world, even the universe.

THE RATIONAL SELF

In the Enlightenment, when science became king, the rational mind was equated with the true self.[1] The goal of human beings came to be the development of the rational mind in pursuit of complete mastery over the world. Technology and science were thought to have the capacity to enlighten humanity and solve the problems of the world.

Again, there is a very biblical dimension to this view of the self. God gave humanity the command to fill the earth and rule it. We are to cultivate and steward the world and all its resources. But there is also a grave temptation toward idolatry here: the idolatry of rationality. The mind's capacity to reason, understand the world and exercise mastery becomes the be-all and end-all. Spock on the original *Star Trek* is a great example of this extreme, in which reason rules, and the imagination, intuition and feelings are repressed or marginalized.

THE ROMANTIC SELF

In rebellion against the rational self, many people turned toward the past, the imagination and poetry to understand the self. Self-expression became the destination and the highest Ideal. Our culture's ongoing commitment to authenticity and being real is rooted in that view of the self.[2]

There is a biblical dimension to this view. Authenticity and transparency are deeply biblical values. How can we ever come into the reality of true community unless we are real with God and one another? But there is also immense temptation toward an idolatry of the romantic self. Self-expression and artistic creativity become the highest ideal, irrespective of the content of the expression. Art becomes a purely subjective reflection of whatever emerges out of our conscious and unconscious mind. Scripture, however, teaches us how fallen we are and how lost, confused and even perverse we will become if we give free rein to self-expression.

The original *Star Trek*'s Dr. McCoy is a great example of the idealistic romantic view of the self. Spock might appropriately ask McCoy, "Did you ever have an emotion you didn't express?"

THE THERAPEUTIC SELF

As Paul Vitz has pointed out, in the modern world psychology has become religion.[3] "Salvation" comes through rational understanding of the self in its conscious and unconscious dimensions. The goal of the self is authentic self-expression. Wholeness and self-fulfillment become the highest ideals. This integration of rational understanding and genuine self-expression combines the rational and romantic visions of the self and applies them to the psyche.

Again, there is a very biblical dimension to this view of the self. Scripture warns us against the darkness in each of our hearts and our temptation toward self-deception. Exploration of the power of the unconscious mind has helped us understand some of the untold truths of the heart. If wholeness is seen as fulfillment of the unique expression of the image of Christ in us, then it is the biblical destination for the self. But if wholeness is merely an experience of self-fulfillment and authentic self-expression, it has become a dangerous idol.

Counselor Deanna Troi on *StarTrek: The Next Generation* is a good image of the therapeutic view of the self.

Idolizing the therapeutic self is probably the most common idolatry among healing ministries. So I want to explore the potential for idolatry here just a bit more.

The drive toward self-fulfillment and authentic self-expression is pervasive in our culture. Often even healing ministries seek God's healing power for very idolatrous ends: total escape from pain and the achievement of complete self-fulfillment. A new ethic may begin to creep into the church or ministry that is seeking healing. It might be termed an ethic of self-fulfillment. Instead of calling people to loving and sometimes suffering servanthood, we promise people healing, fulfillment and self-actualization. We then call people to a supposedly Christian ethic that leaves out the cross. Prayer ministry is especially vulnerable to the temptation to adopt the vision and values of the therapeutic self.

Jesus told us that if we save our life and seek our self-fulfillment, we will lose our life. But if we lose our life for his sake and the gospel, we will find our life. The cross condemns any cult of self-fulfillment.

Prayer ministry is primarily about the cure of the soul. It is a powerful aid in the ongoing process of sanctification, of becoming like Jesus in all we do, think, feel and believe. This process involves personal redemptive suffering, in which we must travel in pain through the valley of emptiness before we experience much healing. And it involves turning outward in other-directed redemptive suffering, serving others sacrificially as Jesus did. Self-fulfillment is a byproduct and not the goal of the ministry of healing.

THE COMMUNAL SELF

Postmodern thinking emphasizes the role of the community in the formation of identity. We are not just autonomous individuals; rather we are persons shaped primarily by the communities we inhabit and the dialogues we carry on.[4] For the postmodern thinker, selves are socially constructed.

There are very biblical dimensions to the communal understanding of the self, and it brings a helpful corrective to the cultural myth of autonomous individualism. The decisive dimension of identity for a Hebrew in biblical times was his or her participation in the people of God. The communal view of self leaves room for the very biblical understanding that the Christian self is developed in relationships and has concrete meaning only in the context of community. Asian, African, Native American and Latino cultures generally understand and honor the corporate dimensions of the self to a much healthier degree than Western culture has tended to.

Nevertheless, in our day the communal self has become an idolatrous self as well. We may see our connection to a community, based on gender, race or sexual orientation, as the one defining element of our identity. We choose to name ourselves, regardless of how God sees and names us. Truly horrifying things have been justified in the name of communal identity throughout history and into the present day.

One expression of an unhealthy communal orientation toward identity is to identify ourselves with an oppressed group and then take on a victim mentality. We then reject responsibility for our own sin and sickness and look outside of ourselves for all "salvation" and wholeness. The victim mentality is possibly the most serious barrier to true healing. If we will not take personal responsibility for what we have done and for the task of developing a healthy self, we will have little hope of ever making progress.

In more traditional cultures we see a different idolatrous tendency: ancestors, parents or past traditions can be idolized, replacing or relativizing God's authority.

The Borg in *Star Trek: The Next Generation* suggests an idolatry of the communal self, though its identity is not rooted in a story of common oppression, like many present-day understandings of the communal self.

TOWARD A CHRISTIAN VIEW OF THE SELF

Each of these cultural views of the self contains an important dimension of the meaning of being made in the image of God. We embrace the biblically consistent dimensions of any particular cultural view, but we also discern how in each case one dimension of humanness has been exalted to a place of idolatry.

A Christian vision, then, is shaped by both Scripture and culture. No other way is truly possible. But we guard the integrity of both Scripture and culture, Spirit and flesh. Once again, the Christian faith is fundamentally incarnational. Even our epistemology—our understanding of how we know what we know—must be genuinely incarnational.

Appendix 2

The Healing Ministry Applied to Ethnic and Racial Identity

With an African American pastor, Brenda Salter McNeil, I have written a book called *The Heart of Racial Justice: How Soul Change Leads to Social Change.* In it we adapt insights from the healing ministry and apply them to ethnic identity formation and racialized relationships. We have personally experienced, and seen many other friends and partners experience, much pain, division, failure and burnout in the ministry of racial reconciliation.

We have asked ourselves, Why has there been so much pain, so many untimely deaths, so many fractured relationships? Why has so much expenditure of money and effort, time and energy, brought so little progress and change? And how do we respond? What is the need of the hour in the ministry of ethnic and racial reconciliation?

In the face of these questions, we looked hard for a new model, a new approach to the battle that will yield a greater return, a few more victories and a few less defeats, and a more hopeful and joyful experience of partnership in ministry. In our search we considered the potential of the ministry of healing. We adapted and applied biblical, pastoral, spiritual and psychological insights of the ministry of healing to the problems of racial and ethnic division and hurt. We are very excited about this model and very encouraged by a growing sense of fruitfulness and blessing as we pursue it.

The healing ministry has been effectively applied to issues of personal identity, sexual brokenness, gender confusion and broken relationships, but not yet to ethnic identity formation and the need for cross-ethnic reconciliation. Further, healing models of the past have been primarily individualistic and not sufficiently applied to corporate issues of conflict, hostility and brokenness.

We long to see individuals reconciled cross-ethnically, and we long to see whole communities reconciled and partnering together with a new level of trust, based on God's presence to heal and to empower ministry in a broken world.

We feel called to the ministry of healing people and nations for the glory of God and the witness of the church in the world. We believe that the emerging generation of leaders will resonate with this calling and be drawn to pursue with us such healing of people and nations.

We propose five key steps that emerge out of a deeply biblical perspective to flesh out a healing model of ethnic reconciliation.

1. *Worship.* We worship God—Father, Son and Holy Spirit—and practice his presence. In so doing we encounter God's presence and power to melt our hearts and create new possibilities for being healed, reconciled, and re-created for partnership in the global ministry of reconciliation.

2. *Affirm our true ethnic identity and renounce false identities.* We understand biblically and embrace personally our God-intended ethnic identity. We also learn to identify and renounce distorted, destructive ethnic identities as the idolatries they are. As we embrace a healthy identity, we are empowered to speak the truth with the goal of hearing, healing and being healed.

3. *Receive and extend forgiveness.* We are all sinners and sinned against and desperately need forgiveness. So together in God's presence we revisit the personal and corporate memories of our sin and of being sinned against. Bringing our collective and personal memories into the presence of Christ leads to acts of extending and receiving forgiveness. This cannot be a superficial transaction: only as evil has been truly named can it be dealt with honestly at the cross. In addition, where possible and appropriate, forgiveness will lead to acts of restitution.

4. *Renounce idols.* Then we can name, unmask and renounce the false gods related to racism and ethnocentrism. We renounce the larger spiritual forces of evil that our mothers and fathers and ethnic groups have followed and too often worshiped and obeyed. These forces and idolatries have controlled and bound us. But just as the cross of Christ brings forgiveness of sin, it also brings freedom from the principalities and powers.

5. *Engage in ongoing partnership.* In Christ we are a new creation, victim and perpetrator, able to embrace and live in the power of the resurrection and the gift of the Spirit. Together we become agents of reconciliation in a divided world. We will be drawn to places like impoverished inner cities and troubled ethnic hotspots to model and minister reconciliation as witnesses to the good news and the power of God. But our ongoing partnerships will not just affect ministry in inner cities and in troubled areas of the world. Suburban churches will look different too. Leadership will become more multiethnic, and partnership relationships between diverse churches will become more common.

We are convinced that God is at work in our day to bring healing to a troubled and divided world. As we draw on the resources of Almighty God for healing and restoration, we will no longer be fighting the battle in our own strength. We will no longer limp along in relationships, prisoners to our past. The Spirit and the joy of God can pervade our partnerships in fresh ways. We *are* a new creation, victim and perpetrator, sinner and sinned against, filled by the Holy Spirit for the remaking of the world into the kingdom of our God. That kingdom will be built in the end by the power of God, but God invites us now into collaboration with him, to taste and see that the Lord is good and that his multiethnic kingdom of justice and love has been inaugurated!

Let us join with God and one another to seek his healing presence for the nations.

Appendix 3

The Leadership Journey in Healing Prayer

Some readers of this book will feel nudged by God to begin to lead others into the ministry of healing. Maybe you will start a prayer ministry in your church or fellowship group. Maybe you will begin to train others in how to listen to God and pray for healing. Maybe you will lead or become part of a small group whose mission is to pray for others for healing. The three components of this appendix will help you enter into leading others to pray for healing, guiding you in how to begin a prayer ministry, how to teach others to pray, and how to teach a biblical ethic for healing ministry.

HOW TO BEGIN A PRAYER MINISTRY

Chapter one of this book began with the story about how Bill Leslie and I worked together to launch a prayer ministry at LaSalle Street Church that continues today, long after he has passed away and I have moved on to other ministries. How can you launch and lead a prayer ministry well, so that it lasts for the long haul and brings God's healing presence to many?

I propose a six-stage process that is adapted from Mark Mittelberg's process of building a contagious church.[1] His process focuses on launching new ministries of evangelism, but it fits launching a new ministry of prayer as well.

Start with prayer! I don't put this in the list as a separate stage, because it is really to be practiced at every step along the way. Cry out to God for the sufferers in your midst. Ask God for wisdom in ministering healing. Trust God to bring mentors and guides who can point you in the needed direction.

Then lead a process that can get your ministry fully involved in praying for the cure of souls. Here is a strategy consisting of six stages.

1. *Begin praying for sufferers yourself.* This will help you and your church more than you can know! It's how Bill Leslie began. When he counseled folk who came to visit in his office, at the end he always offered to pray with them. And since he was open about God's healing in his own life, he often had opportunities to pray healing for others.

2. *Begin to communicate your vision and passion for prayer ministry.* If you are the senior pastor or director of a ministry, choose to express your vision and heart for prayer ministry at least once a month, and use every means you can to get people on board.

Then deepen your passion and urgency by going to Scripture and looking at the healing ministry of Jesus. Jesus proclaimed the kingdom of God and healed the sick. Those two parts of his calling were inseparable.

Bill Leslie looked at the Gospels, visited healing prayer ministries and often shared his story and his heart. He clearly had compassion on suffering people. So when he invited some of us to join him in learning to pray for others, we couldn't wait.

If you aren't the senior pastor or director of your ministry, then use whatever means you have to communicate your heart and vision. In particular, tell stories. Work hard to bring the senior pastor or director on board, because you need that person's support to launch a

churchwide effort or to offer prayer ministry regularly at your services or meetings. Most senior pastors and leaders will be absolutely
delighted to help launch a ministry of healing, especially if you come
in humility and if you avoid the dangers (see chapter seventeen) and
talk through the ethics (see the third section of this appendix) of a
healthy prayer ministry.

What if the senior pastor or leader is not on board or has a lot of
concerns? Ask him or her what process of discussion and exploration
would be most helpful. Is the leader willing to read a book or visit a
local ministry of healing prayer? What are his or her concerns?
Would the leader be open to your starting a small group for people
who are interested? The key for your part is getting started and moving forward at the pace at which the senior pastor or director is willing to go along with you. Without that person's support, the ministry
of healing prayer can remain marginalized.

3. *Appoint a leader for prayer ministry in your group or church.* The
senior pastor or director needs to set the priority and value of prayer
ministry and needs to model praying for others. But that person can't
do it all. If you are a senior pastor or leader, you need a point person
for prayer ministry. Bill Leslie knew that and came to me. That person
needs to have a passion for prayer ministry and some relational and
leadership skills for building a team and leading a ministry. The
prayer champion needs to love praying for people, but he or she also
needs to be good at leading and training others and building a team.
The two of you then become partners in leading your church or ministry into healing and transforming prayer. If you don't have an identified champion working with a supportive senior pastor or leader,
the ministry of healing prayer will never come close to reaching its
potential in your ministry.

4. *Train people in prayer ministry.* Have your point person lead a
class. You can use this book or find another prayer ministry curricu-

lum. Practice praying for others in the class.

I will never forget our times of prayer in the training class at La-Salle Street Church. We prayed for issues of physical sickness, depression, abuse and addiction. We began to minister to the roots and not just the symptoms of our struggles. The bond we formed remains between many of us even to this day, almost twenty years later.

5. Invite the interested people who have taken the course onto a prayer ministry team. Begin to meet monthly and pray for your church, for sufferers in the church and for the right time and place to launch a prayer ministry. At LaSalle Street Church we began training in January and then met monthly after the class ended. For many of us, that team became a primary community.

6. *Establish a time and place to offer prayer ministry to the larger body.* Ministry of healing prayer can be a wonderful addition to the celebration of Communion each week or month. People will come forward as you invite them to be loved through prayer, and as the senior leader, point person and other members of the team speak vulnerably and honestly about how God is ministering healing to them through prayer.

Don't expect the sermon or message titled "Onward Christian Soldiers" to be the ideal setup for inviting people to receive healing! Instead, choose to teach on a passage like Mark 5 as Bill Leslie did, and speak from the heart about your own needs for healing. There will likely be long queues of people seeking the grace of God for the healing you are describing.

At LaSalle we decided that the ripe time to launch the ministry was Mother's Day in May 1986. We were aware that in our society many people suffer especially at holiday times and special celebration events. Family celebrations often generate the greatest joy we experience but also sometimes the deepest pain. Holidays are hard for sufferers. We found Mother's Day to be a very good time to begin.

After the ministry has been launched, gather with the team to celebrate! Tell stories of God at work.

As passion for and participation in prayer ministry increase, redouble your efforts and grow the ministry team. Don't slow down to rest on your laurels, even if things are going well. Long-term commitment as well as vision and passion are required if healing through prayer is to really be established within your church or organization's values and practices. Healing is a lifetime journey and will be best served by a long-term commitment.

A word for campus ministries: I have found over the years that it is crucial for leaders of a campus ministry who want to begin prayer ministry to find a church and a mature leader who will provide some oversight. Youth ministries and campus ministries are especially vulnerable to the pitfalls of becoming problem centered, of letting an immature leader take over and give everyone "words" from God, and of fostering inappropriate levels of intimacy and sharing.

To summarize, how do you lead your church or ministry into the practice of prayer ministry and the experience of healing and the cure of souls? Begin with prayer, with crying out to God for sufferers and for the work of God's Spirit. Then lead a process of growth and change that includes six steps.

Step 1. *Own and model* the value for praying for others. Minister to others in prayer personally.

Step 2. *Communicate and instill* your vision and passion for prayer ministry and for healing. Teach from the Gospels. Get people reading books or attending conferences. Tell your own story, and invite others to tell their stories of healing and the cure of their souls.

Step 3. *Appoint a point person* to lead your prayer ministry. The point person then leads others in steps 4, 5 and 6.

Step 4. *Train* every one you can in prayer ministry.

Step 5. Recruit a prayer ministry *team*.

Step 6. With your team, create *opportunities and events* to pray for others, at services and outside of services.

You may already have the position and influence to initiate and direct a process like this. Start by communicating the need and bringing some people together to discuss this section and this book.

Other readers' situations will be quite different: you may feel you *don't* have the influence to help lead a process like this. What should you do? You could give this book or another resource to your senior pastor or leader and anyone else who is interested in prayer ministry. The senior pastor needs to be on board and to help provide overall leadership. And as you pray, reach out and offer your time and energy to the leaders, God could use you to help bring your church or group into a new day in prayer, healing and the cure of souls.

Wouldn't it be glorious if God renewed your church in ministering his presence and power? It could transform you, your church or ministry, and sufferers in your midst for all eternity!

How to Teach Others to Pray

As you journey into leadership in healing prayer, you will need a simple and easily communicable method for getting other people started. I have found no better training for beginners than John Wimber's five-step healing prayer process. It is simple. You can communicate it in an hour or so, and it will give people enough to begin. Wimber lays out this five-step process in his book with Kevin Springer, *Power Healing*. His process has been tweaked and adapted endlessly. Here's my version.

Wimber summarizes the source of the model in this way: "Each element of the five steps is based on Jesus' method of praying for the sick, though in Scripture these steps are not presented in a systematic and chronological fashion. So the application of scriptural truth, not merely the pattern of my personal experience, is the basis for this method."[2] Scripture doesn't provide many details of Jesus' "method" of healing. Generally it goes like this: People with needs come to him requesting to be healed. Jesus often asks whether they have faith. If so, he commands the healing. He doesn't intercede for healing. He discerns whether the healing is to happen, based on the person's faith and presumably on what God is whispering to him. In John 5:19 Jesus explains to his followers, "I tell you the truth, the Son can do nothing by himself; he can do only what he sees his Father doing, because whatever the Father does the Son also does."

Some people believe that Jesus healed because he was God, the Second Person of the Trinity. We are not God, so we are not meant to undertake a ministry of healing like his. But Luke, for instance, makes it clear that Jesus heals because he goes out to minister full of the Holy Spirit (Luke 4:14). Once again, in the healing ministry as in all else, the Christian faith is an incarnational faith. Jesus violates neither his deity nor his humanity in his ministry of healing. And he gives the ministry of healing to his followers (see Matthew 10:8; Luke 9:1; 10:17, which is significant because the healing and exorcism ministry is given not just to the Twelve but to the Seventy; and John 14:12, where Jesus says that the miracles he does will be done and even surpassed by anyone who has faith in him). The early church continues that ministry of healing, according to the book of Acts.

For Jesus, the healing ministry was a collaboration with the Father as he was filled with the Spirit. The same is true for followers of Jesus. Will some people be more gifted in the ministry than others? Of course. But as with all other gifts, ministries and responsibilities in the body of Christ, most of us can have some part and can collaborate with God in the healing of people.

Most often the healing Jesus ministered was instantaneous. But he had faith, was confident in his authority, was attuned to God the Father in ways that none of us will ever match, and was truly and sacrificially other-oriented. For us, discernment, spiritual authority and servant-hearted character will take time, growing in us gradually. We have to learn the ministry of healing in collaboration with Jesus through the Spirit through trial and error. We are to ask God for authority and discernment and yet walk with sober judgment about our level of faith and insight. Paul exhorts us to such discernment regarding our own faith, authority and giftedness in Romans 12:3: "For by the grace given me I say to every one of you: Do not think of yourself more highly than you ought, but rather think of yourself with sober judgment, in accordance with *the measure of faith* God has given you."

The following prayer process reflects the expectation that God can work in authority and power through your prayers but also leaves room for varying levels of authority, giftedness and discernment.

Step 1: the interview. Answers the question "What is the condition?"

Step 2: the diagnostic decision. Answers the question "What is the cause?"

Step 3: the prayer selection. Answers the question "How should I pray for it?"

Step 4: the prayer engagement. Answers the question "When should I stop praying?"

Step 5: postprayer directions. Answers the question "What should the person do to stay healed?"

As you interview people and pray for them, you will want to listen with your ears to what they are saying and see with your eyes what is happening with them, but you will also want to listen with your heart and spirit to the Spirit of God. So before explaining each step of the prayer process, I want to say a couple of things about how you will hear from God as you pray and how the gift of speaking in tongues might fit into praying for others.

As you begin to listen to God on behalf of others, be attuned to the diversity of ways God can speak. He may use some of the following:

- a Scripture
- an impression
- a nudge or whisper
- a word spelled out in your imagination
- a sense that you have the first word to say and just need to start speaking and the rest will come
- an image or mental picture
- a dream
- a burning in your heart that tells you that you need to say something specific
- a sympathetic pain somewhere in your body letting you know that God wants you to pray for that part of the other person's body
- a strong feeling
- a name
- a song or chorus you are to sing
- a message in an unknown tongue

Often God will speak to you in ways that fit your temperament. If you are a visual artist, God may give you a picture or image. If you are fairly rational, God may suggest a thought or bring a Scripture to mind.

When you have a sense that God may be speaking to you, suggest to the person what you are seeing or sensing, and ask if it makes sense to them. Be cautious about what you claim, especially when you are just learning to hear God for others. Over time you will discover the appropriate level of confidence in what you hear, based on your gifts and your measure of faith.

Don't try to interpret the word or nudge that you hear; just pass it on to the person. When I try to figure out everything I am hearing from God for another, I often get it mixed up. Just yesterday I prayed for a person about her calling and the next steps she needed to take toward it. I sensed that God had led her to a fork in the road and she needed to make a choice that would affect the rest of her life. I also sensed that she would struggle to find courage to make the more challenging but ultimately more profoundly healing choice. Now I thought *I* knew what the choice was, but all I really got from God was a sense that she had to make a choice. So I left my interpretation unexpressed.

Almost immediately she began to hear from God herself. She knew just what the choice was and what she had to do. She prayed and wept for joy to think that God had spoken to her so personally. And here's the important part: the choice she needed to make was not at all what I had expected. Fortunately, I had only stated what I sensed from God and had held back from saying what I thought it meant. She thus had room to hear from God herself and experienced a powerful word.

This time I held back. Other times I have said too much and interrupted what God might otherwise have done.

THE GIFT OF TONGUES

Scripture seems to point to three different uses for the gift of tongues. First, at Pentecost God used the apostles' speaking in many tongues to proclaim the wonders of God and evangelize people (Acts 2). Missionary friends have recounted experiences that are similar, when God used a missionary to speak in a language she or he didn't know in order to bring the gospel to a place where it had never been known. Second, God uses people with the gift of tongues to edify the people of God (1 Corinthians 14:12). Someone will speak aloud a message in an unknown language when the Christian community is gathered together, and someone will interpret. Often the message is very simple, about God's love or nurture or assurance. But somehow, because it has been spoken in another tongue, the message enters more deeply into the hearts of believers. Finally, in 1 Corinthians 13:1 Paul writes of speaking in the tongues "of men" and "of angels," and later he suggests that people who pray in tongues pray with their spirit but not their mind (1 Corinthians 14:14), in order to edify themselves (1 Corinthians 14:4). Here he seems to suggest that people might use tongues personally and devotionally to pray with their spirit. The Corinthians had the problem of being superspiritual and of praying far too often with their spirit and not their mind, so Paul calls them to restore balance and pray more with their mind. I suggest that today, however, people often pray too much with their mind and far too little with their spirit, so we need to restore the balance in the other direction.

For many of us, tongues operates in this third way. We pray whatever syllables come to our mouth, prompted by our feelings or spirit. This practice seems to attune us to God. That is why I pray in tongues privately, under my breath, whenever I pray for others.

I believe the gift of tongues is like all other gifts. Almost all of us can speak in tongues in some measure, just as almost all of us can study the Bible, hear from God, share our faith, and teach and lead others to some degree. When we have a particular gift, it means we operate in it more consistently, with greater power and impact. But even if we don't have that gift, we still participate in the activity at some level if we are willing and choose to do so. On this basis I have come to the conviction that some level of experience in speaking in tongues, at least personally and devotionally, is available to everyone. Some operate more powerfully, and in a gifted way, with tongues— or prophecy or evangelism or leadership or healing. But all can have some experience in each of these ministries, as the Spirit works.

Of course, speaking in tongues is not a more powerful or important gift than others. Paul seems to rank it lower than gifts that use both mind and spirit, and he certainly ranks it lower than character qualities like love. So if you don't agree with me and choose not to pursue speaking in tongues, God can still use you to pray for others. But many of us have found speaking in tongues to be a very helpful way to connect to our own spirit and the Spirit of God, especially within very rational and materialistic cultural contexts. If you want to learn to speak in tongues, find someone who speaks in tongues and has helped others do so. When I help others learn this practice, I ask them to especially confess any sexual sins and any past involvement in the occult (e.g., Ouija boards, ESP). There are good spirits and bad. I pray for them to be filled with the Holy Spirit and have them confess Jesus as Lord. Then I lay hands on them, have them ask God for the gift of speaking in tongues and encourage them to speak whatever syllables come from their heart. It is not a rational experience but an emotional or spiritual one, just as Paul says. Many people wait for some automatic and overwhelming event. Sometimes that happens. Far more often, however, it is like beginning to use any gift. The first steps can be halting and awkward. But with practice, praying the syllables that come from our hearts after we have asked to be filled with the Holy Spirit can become a regular and helpful part of our devotional lives and our listening prayer practices.

Now let's get specific about the steps of the prayer process. The following section is adapted from the steps outlined in John Wimber and Kevin Springer's fine book *Power Healing*. I encourage you to get that book if you want to explore this more.

1. The Interview

We begin with the question, *"'Where does it hurt?'* I ask, 'What do you want me to pray for?' I listen on two levels: the natural level and the supernatural level."[3] On a natural level I am listening to the problem and to the emotional intensity of the person. I focus on what Scripture has to say, and also with what I know about the person, especially the person's patterns and past. I am also listening for issues that I have prayed for before.

On a spiritual level, I am attuned to the different ways the Spirit might be speaking or nudging me to pray. I am listening to God for insight into the problem, or into the roots of the problem. Often people will share symptoms of their problem, but God will nudge me to ask a question about the roots of the problem. Words of wisdom and words of knowledge and discernment of spirits are the spiritual gifts I am often leaning on at this point in the healing prayer procedure. That listening then can lead to the next step.

2. The Diagnostic Decision

In this step I seek to identify and clarify "the root of the person's problem. *The diagnostic decision answers the question, 'Why does this person have this condition?'* This is a crucial step in the healing prayer procedure, because it determines the type of prayer needed to bring healing."[4]

I have found that sometimes the person describes the root problem and we can go right into prayer for exactly what the person has requested. Other times, I find that God nudges me to pray in a way that goes deeper or in a different direction than what the person requested. Throughout, I seek to honor the person and what they have requested. But I have also discovered that often the most deeply moving times in prayer are ones in which God leads me to pray in ways the person didn't expect or request.

Most people think they are unable to discern these causes or hear from God in these ways, especially when they are just beginning to learn to pray for others. I certainly have experienced a huge learning

curve when it comes to hearing from God and praying for others as
God nudges. The most crucial factor in my growth has been practice
and more practice. In addition, I have learned to ask others what
connected for them and why when I pray for them, so that each time
I pray, I learn a little more. The key then is often not training in psychology or medicine, though such training can be helpful, but rather
growth in listening to God as I pray for others.[5]

3. The Prayer Selection

We now move to the next step and ask, "*What kind of prayer is needed
to help this person?*' What lies behind this question is an even more
fundamental question: what does God want to do at this particular
time for this person?"[6] God may want to heal them right then, but I
find I usually need to ask for discernment. God often wants to bring
some kind of healing, but not always the kind of healing that the person is asking for at that moment.

God is the healer. We collaborate with God in the healing moment
and process. So hearing what God wants to do at that moment is one
crucial dimension of practicing prayer for others in the power of the
Spirit. God will communicate to our hearts that he wants to heal, and
how specifically he will heal, and then our hearts and words agree
with God. We speak into the present what we have sensed God wants
us to declare about what God is doing. God delights to work in co-
operation with us in this way as we listen to God's whispers.[7]

4. The Prayer Engagement

In the step of prayer engagement we ask ourselves, "*How effective are
our prayers?*' The prayer engagement consists of prayer, laying on of
hands, and, when needed, further interviewing. The way we pray is
determined by our diagnostic decision and prayer selection."[8]

I will first ask people if I can lay hands on them and pray. Then, after laying on hands, I pray aloud asking the Holy Spirit to come and minister to the person. My prayers are quite direct and simple: "Holy Spirit, come. Holy Spirit, show us what you are doing and how you want to heal. Holy Spirit, lead me as I pray.

In *Power Healing*, John Wimber reminds us there are four areas that divine healing may be applied to: the spirit, the effects of past hurts, the body and demonization.

There are several indications that it is time to stop praying. Often the Holy Spirit will remove his power, or he will give me a sense of deep peace that I have prayed for all that I am supposed to pray for. I find that so many people who pray for others feel like they have to add more words whenever there is silence. Sheer number of words never brought healing to anyone. And sometimes adding extra words can even begin to undo the healing God is bringing by blurring the focus of what God is doing.

At other times those being prayed for indicate that they have received from God what they hoped for. Finally, I end the session when I have run out of ideas or no longer sense any direction from the Holy Spirit about what to pray for, or the person seems shut down from making any more progress.

5. Post-prayer Directions

In the last step we ask ourselves, *"What should this person do to remain healed?" and "What should this person do if he or she was not healed?"*[9] When people are not healed or appear to have given up, I remind them that God is still present and suggest that now or later they receive more prayer, often recommending "soaking prayer," administered by a team committed to a longer and more gradual progress.

When applicable, I tell people who have received healing related to sinful patterns of activity to sin no more (see John 8:11). I also encourage everyone who has received healing to keep practicing the spiritual disciplines that will help them remain filled with God's presence and receive grace for a whole and holy life. Beyond their own private practice of these spiritual disciplines, people need to live within the context of overall pastoral care, honest conversation, and accountability through involvement in a church congregation and in a small group.

May God give you wisdom and power as you begin to teach others to pray! Hopefully this short introduction will get you started.

HOW TO TEACH AN ETHIC FOR HEALING PRAYER

In the leadership journey we need to orient people with guidelines, boundaries and ethics of praying for others. What are appropriate boundaries and guidelines for the use of this kind of emotional and spiritual power? Let me suggest a few.

1. The goal of prayer ministry is to love others well, and the measure of success or failure is whether or not people have been loved and honored well. Of course, honoring and loving people will sometimes involve challenging their sin and self-centeredness. But the goal of loving people well by seeking their wholeness in Christ is always to be kept uppermost in view.

2. Leaders of prayer ministries need to be in community and accountability with someone who has insight into the temptations and potential misuses of power in such ministry. This mentor or guide cannot serve under the leadership of the leader. The mentor needs to have the freedom to speak the truth without fear of losing his or her ministry. In addition, prayer ministry leaders need to provide for oversight of and accountability for those they lead.

3. Generally, same-sex prayer ministry is preferable. If cross-gender prayer is needed, such as when men need healing of mother wounds or women need healing of father wounds, a team of a man and a woman ministering together is best.

4. Establish guidelines for appropriate sharing and vulnerability. Members of churches that become too focused on prayer ministry can become problem centered, inward and inappropriately revealing in public situations. In general, issues of sexual, relational and emotional struggle should be shared in relatively private and intimate contexts.

5. Be honest about what level of confidentiality sufferers can expect. If they tell you something they have done that is illegal, you are responsible to report them. Also, sufferers may need to know that prayer ministers are under supervision and may need to share confidential information with the supervisor.

6. Validate different styles and approaches to prayer ministry. Avoid establishing one style of praying (such as expressive) or one approach (such as charismatic) as the "right" way to pray for sufferers.

7. Integrate prophetic people into your ministry in healthy and well-supervised ways. Do not let young, immature people who have "prophetic words" and gifting hijack the ministry and create havoc. If a "prophetic" confrontational person does not follow direction and leadership well, he or she cannot be in the ministry. In general, prophet types need to be supervised and led by pastor types.

8. Set appropriate expectations. As the pastor at the church where I first led prayer ministry would often say, "Come receive prayer. You will have an experience of being profoundly loved, and that's not so bad, is it? And you might hear the Master's voice saying to you, 'Go in peace, my son, my daughter. Your faith has made you well.'" He never overpromised results.

9. Call people to maturity, not dependency or submission to your authority. Again, prayer leaders must be in supervisory relationships so that they don't deceive themselves at this point. If you are a prayer minister, send prayer seekers to other ministers after you have prayed with them several times. Graduate them. Do not give into the temp-

tation to run their lives. If you are a sufferer, after a reasonable period of receiving prayer, choose to move into a new phase of turning outward and giving to others. The period of receiving will depend on the severity of your need. But it may well be that you can begin to turn outward and care for others sooner than you expect.

A good summary statement: Common sense is absolutely crucial for prayer ministry! Unfortunately, sometimes common sense is undervalued in these ministries. Value it, seek it out, pursue practical wisdom and insight for the cure of the souls in your care.

An overarching imperative: Love others well! That's really the bottom line of any prayer session, not how dramatic or supercharged it was.

These guidelines are a good beginning. As they are validated in your ministry and as you discover other rules of the road, you may want to type them all up and give them to every person who prays for others in your ministry. These boundaries free people to love others in healthy ways through prayer. Hopefully you won't need to be healed from your involvement in a ministry of healing, as I did at one point. May these hard-earned lessons help you avoid the pitfalls and experience the great adventure of learning to collaborate with God and love others through healing prayer.

For Further Reading

Barfield, Owen. *Poetic Diction*. Middletown, Conn.: Wesleyan University Press, 1973.

Bergner, Mario. *Setting Love in Order: Hope and Healing for the Homosexual*. Grand Rapids: Baker, 1995.

Bellah, Robert, et al. *Habits of the Heart*. New York: Harper & Row, 1985.

Bevan, Edwyn. *Symbolism and Belief*. London: G. Allen and Unwin, 1938.

Bowlby, John. *Attachment*. New York: Basic Books, 1969.

———. *Loss*. New York: Basic Books, 1973.

———. *A Secure Base*. New York: Basic Books, 1988.

Buber, Martin. *I and Thou*. Trans. Walter Kaufmann. New York: Scribner, 1970.

The Book of Common Prayer. New York: Church Hymnal Corporation, 1979.

Cloud, Henry, and John Townsend. *Boundaries*. Grand Rapids, Mich.: Zondervan, 1992.

Dalbey, Gordon. *Healing the Masculine Soul*. Waco, Tex.: Word, 1988.

———. *Sons of the Father*. Wheaton, Ill.: Tyndale House, 1992.

Gergen, Kenneth. *The Saturated Self*. New York: Basic Books, 1991.

Green, Garret. *Imagining God*. Grand Rapids: Eerdmans, 1998.

Howatch, Susan. *Glamorous Powers*. New York: Alfred A. Knopf, 1988.

Lewis, C. S. *Mere Christianity*. 1952. Reprint, San Francisco: Harper & Row, 1980.

———. *Miracles*. New York: Macmillan, 1947.

————. *Perelandra.* New York: Simon & Schuster, 1996.

————. *That Hideous Strength.* New York: Simon & Schuster, 1996.

————. *Till We Have Faces.* New York: Harcourt, 1956.

————. *The Weight of Glory.* New York: Macmillan, 1949.

Mulholland, M. Robert. *Invitation to a Journey.* Downers Grove, Ill.: InterVarsity Press, 1993.

Nouwen, Henri. *Life of the Beloved.* New York: Crossroad, 1992.

————. *The Way of the Heart.* San Francisco: Harper & Row, 1981.

Otto, Rudolf. *The Idea of the Holy.* Trans. John Harvey. 2nd ed. New York: Oxford University Press, 1970.

Payne, Leanne. *The Healing Presence.* Westchester, Ill.: Crossway, 1989.

————. *Listening Prayer.* Grand Rapids: Baker, 1994.

————. *Real Presence.* Wheaton, Ill.: Crossway, 1988.

————. *Restoring the Christian Soul Through Healing Prayer.* Wheaton, Ill.: Crossway, 1991.

Peterson, Eugene. *A Long Obedience in the Same Direction.* Rev. ed. Downers Grove, Ill.: InterVarsity Press, 2000.

Richardson, Rick. *Evangelism Outside the Box.* Downers Grove, Ill.: InterVarsity Press, 2000.

Rinker, Rosalind. *Prayer: Conversing with God.* Grand Rapids: Zondervan, 1959.

Sanford, Agnes. *The Healing Light.* 1972. Reprint, New York: Ballantine, 1983.

Smalley, Gary, and John Trent. *The Blessing.* Nashville: Thomas Nelson, 1986.

Taylor, Charles. *Sources of the Self.* Cambridge, Mass.: Harvard University Press, 1989.

Trevethan, Thomas. *The Beauty of God's Holiness.* Downers Grove, Ill.: InterVarsity Press, 1985.

Vitz, Paul. *Psychology as Religion.* 2nd ed. Grand Rapids: Eerdmans, 1994.

Webber, Robert. *Ancient-Future Faith.* Grand Rapids: Baker, 1999.

Willard, Dallas. *Hearing God.* 3rd ed. Downers Grove, Ill.: InterVarsity Press, 1999.

————. *The Spirit of the Disciplines.* San Francisco: Harper & Row, 1988.

Wimber, John, with Kevin Springer. *Power Healing.* San Francisco: Harper & Row, 1987.

Wright, N. T. *The New Testament and the People of God.* Minneapolis: Fortress, 1992.

Notes

Chapter 1: Invitation to the Healing Journey
[1]Philip Yancey, "Miracle on LaSalle Street," *Christianity Today*, November 8, 1993, p. 96.
[2]Robert Bly, *The Sibling Society* (Reading, Mass.: Addison-Wesley, 1996).

Chapter 2: What Is Healing?
[1]I want to make it clear that I am not lumping all TV evangelists together here. For instance, I recently watched Reinhard Bonnke and Benny Hinn proclaiming the gospel, ministering healing and sharing their vision for reaching nations. In that session their ministry and vision were healthy and inspiring!
[2]For this phrasing I'm indebted to a sermon by Rebecca Pippert about the meaning of the cross.
[3]Discerning readers may notice the parallel between my definition of healing and Robert Mulholland's definition of spiritual growth in his *Invitation to a Journey* (Downers Grove, Ill.: InterVarsity Press, 1993).

Chapter 3: A Map for the Journey
[1]Many thanks to my dad, who told this story to my brothers and me. It lives on for my kids now!

Chapter 4: The Healing Presence of God
[1]St. Augustine, quoted by Leanne Payne, *The Healing Presence* (Westchester, Ill.: Crossway, 1989), p. 131.
[2]C. S. Lewis, *The Weight of Glory and Other Essays,* ed. Walter Hooper (New York: Collier, 1975), pp. 3-4.
[3]C. S. Lewis, *Miracles* (New York: Macmillan, 1960), p. 92.
[4]Payne, *Healing Presence*, p. 27.

Chapter 5: Practicing God's Healing Presence
[1]Garrett Green, *Imagining God: Theology and the Religious Imagination* (Grand Rapids: Eerdmans, 1989), p. 84
[2]Rudolf Otto, *The Idea of the Holy,* trans. John Harvey (1923; reprint, New York: Oxford University Press, 1970), p. 158.
[3]Ibid., pp. 141-42.

[4]Leanne Payne, *The Healing Presence* (Westchester, Ill.: Crossway, 1989), p. 131.
[5]Leanne Payne, *Real Presence* (Wheaton, Ill.: Crossway, 1979), pp. 148-49.
[6]Rosalind Rinker, *Prayer: Conversing with God* (Grand Rapids: Zondervan, 1959), p. 23.
[7]C. S. Lewis, *Mere Christianity* (1952; reprint, San Francisco: Harper & Row, 1980), p. 198.

Chapter 6: Hearing God's Whisper
[1]Dallas Willard, *Hearing God,* 2nd ed. (Downers Grove, Ill.: InterVarsity Press, 1999), p. 22.
[2]Ibid., p. 178, quoting G. Campbell Morgan.

Chapter 7: Understanding Gender Identity
[1]For an alternative interpretation of the relationship between creation and the Fall, see Mary Stewart Van Leeuwen, *Gender and Grace: Love, Work and Parenting in a Changing World* (Downers Grove, Ill.: InterVarsity Press, 1990), pp. 33-52. For Van Leeuwen, both men and women were called together to accountable dominion *and* sociability. Only in the Fall did they begin to focus on different extremes. Men have tended to turn interdependent accountable dominion into male domination. And women have tended to turn sociability into enmeshment, abandoning their responsibility for accountable dominion. Jesus' teachings and redemption, and the gift of the Holy Spirit at Pentecost, begin to restore interdependent accountable dominion and sociability to both men and women, in partnership. At this point, I tend to root more of the differences between men and women in creation than Van Leeuwen does. But I am quite concerned, as she is, about the injustice that this view has often led people into.
[2]Ibid.
[3]C. S. Lewis, *Perelandra* (New York: Simon & Schuster, 1996), especially the great dance in Paradise near the end; Leanne Payne, *The Healing Presence* (Westchester, Ill.: Crossway, 1989), p. 128; Karl Stern, *Flight from Woman* (New York: Paragon House, 1985).
[4]Payne, *Healing Presence,* p. 128.
[5]Edwyn Bevan, *Symbolism and Belief* (London: G. Allen and Unwin, 1938), pp. 335-36.
[6]For more on metaphors and images as bridges between concepts and feelings, see especially C. S. Lewis's *Miracles,* particularly the chapter titled "Horrid Red Things."
[7]Thanks to Leanne Payne, who first led me through these prayers for the cleansing of the imagination.

Chapter 8: Embracing Our Real Identity
[1]C. S. Lewis, *Till We Have Faces* (New York: Harcourt Brace, 1957), p. 294.
[2]Leanne Payne, *The Healing Presence* (Westchester, Ill.: Crossway, 1989), p 21.
[3]Some commentators would critique this view that Paul's phrase "new creation" refers to us as individuals. They interpret 2 Corinthians 5:17 as Paul's conviction that when we are in Christ, we have *entered into* the new creation, the kingdom or rule of God that Jesus inaugurated. This new creation is primarily a corporate reality, they would assert. I don't think the distinction is very meaningful, for both corporate and individual interpretations of this passage clearly fit into Paul's thinking. We are a new creation individually because of our union with Christ. And we have also entered into the larger reality of the new creation, the Jesus-inaugurated kingdom of God.

Chapter 9: Renouncing Unreal Identities

[1]Leanne Payne, *The Healing Presence* (Westchester, Ill.: Crossway, 1989), pp. 52-59.

[2]Mario Bergner, lecture in the course of his Redeemed Lives program (see <www .redeemedlives.org>).

[3]Ibid.

Chapter 10: The Dialogue with Mother and Father

[1]Martin Buber, *I and Thou*, trans. Walter Kaufmann (New York: Scribner, 1970), pp. 53-54.

[2]These ideas about being and well-being are well supported by the work of John Bowlby on attachment theory. See John Bowlby, *A Secure Base* (New York: Basic Books, 1988). "For a person to know that an attachment figure [elsewhere mother-figure] is available and responsive gives him a strong and pervasive feeling of security, and so encourages him to value and continue the relationship" (p. 27).

[3]For more on God's blessing, see Gordon Dalbey, *Healing the Maculine Soul* (Waco, Tex.: Word, 1988).

[4]To explore the power of blessing and the ways that fathers blessed their children in Scripture, Gary Smalley and John Trent's book *The Blessing* (Nashville: Thomas Nelson, 1986), is quite helpful. They identify five dimensions of blessing: meaningful touch, a spoken message, attaching high value to the one being blessed, picturing a special future for the one being blessed, and an active commitment to fulfill the blessing.

Chapter 11: Healing Mother Wounds

[1]Again, attachment theory has been invaluable for understanding the causes of increased anxiety whenever a child is separated from the mother figure. "Man, like other animals, responds with fear to certain situations, not because they carry a high risk of pain and danger, but because they signal an increase of risk" (John Bowlby, *A Secure Base* [New York: Basic Books, 1988], p. 30).

[2]C. S. Lewis, *Miracles* (New York: Macmillan, 1960), p. 94.

[3]Thomas Trevethan, *The Beauty of God's Holiness* (Downers Grove, Ill.: InterVarsity Press, 1995), pp. 223-24.

[4]The following steps in prayer reflect my own prayer process as experienced at a Pastoral Care Ministry conference led by Leanne Payne.

Chapter 12: Healing Father Wounds

[1]For more on boundaries and what happens when they are violated, see Henry Cloud and John Townsend, *Boundaries* (Grand Rapids: Zondervan, 1992).

[2]See Gordon Dalbey, *Sons of the Father* (Wheaton, Ill.: Tyndale House, 1992), pp. 6-7, especially in relation to men, and in relation to women on pp. 17-19.

[3]For more on being the Beloved, see Henri Nouwen, *Life of the Beloved* (New York: Crossroad, 1992).

[4]Though Jesus had not yet begun public ministry and therefore had not "earned" God's pleasure through his accomplishments, he had made some very significant choices. In his wilderness temptation he had passed the test not to use his power for himself, and he had chosen to identify with sinful Israel by receiving John's baptism of repentance. I think the point can still

identify with sinful Israel by receiving John's baptism of repentance. I think the point can still be made that through our choice to identify with Jesus, we too receive God's pleasure and blessing before we have done anything at all to earn it.

Chapter 13: Forgiveness and Healing Memories
[1]Agnes Sanford, *The Healing Light* (1972; reprint, New York: Ballantine, 1983), pp. 118-19.
[2]Lewis Smedes, *Forgive and Forget* (San Francisco: Harper & Row, 1984).

Chapter 14: Battling Sexual Addiction
[1]Leanne Payne, *The Healing Presence* (Westchester, Ill.: Crossway, 1989), p. 197.
[2]Dennis Prager, "Judaism, Homosexuality and Civilization," *Ultimate Issues* 6, no. 2 (1990): 3.
[3]*The Book of Common Prayer* (New York: Church Hymnal Corporation, 1979), pp. 302-3.

Chapter 15: Healing, Sacraments and Touch
[1]You can find the ancient prayers for blessing water in Leanne Payne's *Restoring the Christian Soul Through Healing Prayer* (Wheaton, Ill.: Crossway, 1991), pp. 164-65.
[2]Robert Webber, *Ancient-Future Faith* (Grand Rapids: Baker, 1999), pp. 148-49.

Chapter 16:
[1]Rick Richardson, *Evangelism Outside the Box* (Downers Grove, Ill.: InterVarsity Press, 2000).

Chapter 17: Dangers and Dead Ends on the Healing Journey
[1]See Susan Howatch, *Glamorous Powers* (New York: A.A. Knopf, 1988).
[2]Mario Bergner, *Setting Love in Order* (Grand Rapids: Baker, 1995), p. 94.

Appendix 1: On Biblical and Cultural Sources of the Self
[1]For more on the rational and romantic views of the self, see Charles Taylor, *Sources of the Self* (Cambridge, Mass.: Harvard University Press, 1989).
[2]For more on the romantic and individualistic view of the self, see Robert Bellah et al., *Habits of the Heart* (New York: Harper & Row, 1985).
[3]For more on the therapeutic self, see Paul Vitz, *Psychology as Religion,* 2nd ed. (Grand Rapids: Eerdmans, 1994).
[4]For more on postmodern selves, see Kenneth Gergen, *The Saturated Self* (New York: Basic-Books, 1991).

Appendix 3: The Leadership Journey in Healing Prayer
[1]For more, see Mark Mittelberg, *Building Contagious Churches* (Grand Rapids: Zondervan, 2000).
[2]John Wimber and Kevin Springer, *Power Healing* (San Francisco: Harper & Row, 1987), p. 198.
[3]Ibid., p. 199.
[4]Ibid., pp. 199-200.
[5]I hope you will also have gotten insight in discerning root causes as you read this book, especially in the chapters starting with "The Dialogue with Mother and Father."

[6]Wimber and Springer, *Power Healing,* p. 204.
[7]You can get more help on listening prayer in chapter two, "Hearing God's Whispering Voice."
[8]Wimber and Springer, *Power Healing,* p. 211.
[9]Ibid., p. 235.

RICK RICHARDSON
Associate National Director for Evangelism
for InterVarsity Christian Fellowship.

Rick has been in campus ministry for twenty years and regularly speaks and ministers on campuses in many different parts of the country. Rick is also an ordained priest with the Anglican Mission in America, and served for three years as pastor of evangelism and small groups for Church of the Resurrection in Wheaton, Illinois. Rick received his M.Div. from Northern Baptist Seminary and is presently working on a Ph.D. in intercultural studies at Trinity Evangelical Divinity School.

Rick's book *Evangelism Outside the Box: New Ways to Help People Experience the Good News* has been widely used by campus ministries, by Emergent churches and in seminary classes on evangelism. He has also published four Bible discussion guides for seekers and skeptics: *Sex, Spirituality, Finding God* and *Following God.* With Brenda Salter McNeil, Rick is the coauthor of *The Heart of Racial Justice: How Soul Change Leads to Social Change* (IVP). Rick seeks to bring together his passions for evangelism, prayer and racial reconciliation in order to cast vision and to equip an emerging postmodern generation in ministry for the sake of the gospel of Jesus Christ.

If you would like to contact Rick, you can e-mail him at Rick_Richardson@ivstaff.org.